What a way to run a country, eh?
Thanks a lot Meghan Markle!

January

The year started with man-of-the-people Boris 'M̶ ̶ ̶ ̶ ̶ ̶ ̶ ̶ ̶ 'y Mail column on how dreadful it is that under woke ̶ ̶ ̶ ̶ ̶ ̶ 's no longer allowed to burn one's Christmas tree in o̶ ̶ ̶ ̶

Does he know anyone who doesn't live in a mansi̶ ̶ ̶ ̶

If he had just searched the internet for whether you s̶ ̶ ̶ ̶ ̶ ̶ ̶istmas tree in the fire, he would have seen that you should not, due to the very ̶ ̶ ̶ ̶ ̶ger you might burn your house down owing to the intense heat created by the sap of a fir.

Specifically, a chimney sweep's website says, "Your Christmas tree is not appropriate fuel for your fireplace, and burning it can create a blaze that is unpredictable and difficult to control."

Unpredictable and difficult to control - which flaming chump ex-Prime Minister does that remind you of?

The current PM, Tetchy Sunak, was found to have considered the Tories' Rwanda plan a giant waste of money when he used to be Chancellor. Too expensive, not good value for money and wouldn't deter people from crossing, he thought.

This came to light when papers from the time were released, which must have come as a shock to Prime Minister Tetchy, as he now claimed that the Rwanda plan was his number one priority.

It's almost as though the requirement to be the leader of the Conservative Party is that you don't have any principles other than self-advancement.

That, and being odd.

Titchi Sunak was permanently awkward looking in the company of non-millionaires and he could'nt talk to ordinary people without coming over weird.

King Charles is properly weird, from a weird family and had a weird upbringing, but even he looked less strained in other people's company than that stick insect of mendacity that was the Drear Leader.

You recall that Tetchy asked a homeless person whether they were in business, presumably because he couldn't think of anything else to say to someone he hadn't met before, and he didn't know how to use a credit card, waving it around as though it was magic wand, but all the evidence points to him not being a wizard.

He was, however, our Prime Minister as the year began. What could possibly go wrong?

In health news, NHS junior doctors were on strike.

Ex-Tory MP Edwina Currie felt unconstrained by it not being her business any longer and announced that those doctors on the picket lines did not care about their patients.

Presumably, the thinking goes: they dreamed of being a doctor at school and they took the right courses and worked hard to get the results they needed to go to university and study their faces off while racking up massive debts for doing so, only to fall in love with money and stop believing in the thing they had dedicated their whole life to doing and ceased to care about patients.

That must sound very believable to the sort of person that used to be a Conservative MP.

Edwina Currie said junior doctors should feel valued by the "smiles on the faces of those people that they're able to help" and "not by looking at their pay packet".

She actually said that out loud.

If we paid MPs in smiles, they'd starve to death.

This is the same Edwina Currie who said, "good Christian people don't get AIDS", the same Edwina Currie who rubber stamped the appointment of Jimmy Savile as Chairman of Broadmoor Psychiatric Hospital, the same Edwina Currie who said that northerners die of "ignorance and chips".

She used to be the Health Secretary!

The cost of giving Junior Doctors the 35% pay rise they wanted was about £1bn. Before the strike, the government had already spent £2bn on refusing to reach a deal and £8bn a year on a tax cut that only the richest 4% of Britons pay.

Junior Doctors wanted salaries to go from £15 an hour to £20 an hour.

By contrast, an electrician charges £90 for an hour of their time and a garage mechanic £60 an hour, so £20 an hour for someone who could save your life didn't seem unreasonable to anyyone except the people in charge who could make that happen.

In other news of worker discontent, teachers of the lefty activist type were threatening strike action over their declining pay and worsening working conditions. The government responded by proposing to recruit teachers from abroad to fill the gaps caused by British teachers giving up on the profession.

Paying British teachers more and improving their working conditions to retain them being not an option.

That would be giving in to socialism! Much better to spend more and import some other country's teachers instead.

In an ideal world, the entire government should have to stay after class for a damn good thrashing.

On the environment, there was discord.

A former Conservative minister announced he was resigning as an MP in protest at the party's dash for oil and gas.

Chris Skidmore, described as a leading voice within the Tory party on green issues, said he would resign from parliament over Fishi Sunak's bill to allow new oil and gas licences to be issued.

A cynic might think this sounded a little surprising, that an MP, a Tory one at that, would take a principled stand and relinquish the power that comes from being a Member of Parliament over an issue close to their hearts.

A quick peek at how he had voted on environmental issues as an MP revealed that Chris Skidmore generally voted against measures to prevent climate change, consistently voted for selling England's state owned forests and generally voted against financial incentives for low carbon emission electricity generation methods.

He also consistently voted against higher taxes on banks and voted against a bankers' bonus tax.

He was also one of the Britannia Unchained lot. The book that explained what a bunch of bone-idle slackers we Brits are.

That was the book that informed the exploding Liz Truss premiership.

And now he declared he could stand it no longer and resigned his seat. One small detail: his seat was going to be abolished anyway a few months later and divided into two. In normal times, they would still be safe Tory seats, but these were not normal times.

In happy coincidence news, Tim 'Catweazle' Martin, out of Wetherspoons, received a knighthood from the very same Conservative Party to which he had donated a large amount of money.

He was one of the most vocal supporters of Brexit from the business community and at least had the decency to stick around after the vote, while his be-knighted contemporaries fled to tax havens abroad.

Other publicans were not impressed, however.

Tom McNeeney, who runs the Oxford pub in Rochdale said, "It's sad. Over the last 15 years or so we've seen the businessman take over the trade of a traditional landlady or landlord. Tim Martin is the poster boy."

Not a poster that anyone would want on their wall, though. No offence.

A poll was taken on how the public feel about the government.

Survey said: badly.

Just one per cent of voters believed Rishi Sunak's administration is "very honest", which goes to show that you can fool at least 1% of the public all of the time.

It was the eyes wasn't it? Those sad "don't hurt me" puppy-dog eyes. That and the skinny suits that make him look like he might snap in half on a windy day.

Asked to what extent, if at all, they would describe the current Government as being either honest, or corrupt, 57% of voters said they would describe them as being corrupt. I'm no expert but that sounds like a majority to me.

Worse than that though - 70% of voters say they are inclined to believe that all politicians in Westminster are "in it for themselves". That's the Boris Effect.

In an effort to rekindle the love of the people, Tetchy went to Stockport to meet local activists.

The voters of that manor turned out to holler their support by asking him to re-sign as Prime

Minister.

Or they may have been shouting "re-sign".

For his comfort, Sunak was hurried in and out so fast that the sound of disapproval failed to catch up with him.

"Leave now", yelled the good people of Stockport, and he left the area but not the job. Yet.

In happier news, NatWest's chairman Sir Howard Davies, a man whose company is in the money lending game, warned of 'easy access' to credit. He also said that he believed it was not currently "that difficult" for people to get on the housing ladder.

That's true. All you need to do is become the chairman of a major bank, be awarded £750,000 a year for being so good as to come to work and you could afford a house or two yourself. Simple.

In related news, while the government was denying pay rises to those people that keep the country safe and well, they were looking forward to a 7.1% salary increase for themselves, which would take them from £86,584 to £92,731 per year, plus expenses, plus pension, plus subsidised everything all of the time.

They're worth it, you see.

The Mirror asked its readers: Do MPs deserve a pay rise?

Yes, said 3% of respondents. No, replied the remaining 97%.

The people had spoken and were ignored in the same instant.

The weather, depending on your location, featured droughts, storms, floods, thawing, freezing and newsworthy climate related events of unprecedented ferocity.

Throughout the year, the word 'unprecedented' was used an unprecedented number of times.

The House of Commons discussed dentistry. Labour said they wanted mandatory supervised teeth brushing for three to five-year-olds.

During the debate, former cabinet minister and senior Conservative MP Andrea Leadsom said: "The opposition's motion talks about supervised toothbrushing for three to five-year-olds. I do not know whether they do not know this, but we have teeth from before we are born."

In fact, she said, when a child is three, their teeth are about four-and-a-half years old.

This means that children's teeth start growing before they are conceived.

She did not know whether we knew that.

A new report concluded that Brexit would leave the country £311bn worse off by the middle of the next decade and had already cost the economy of the UK £140bn.

Sadiq Khan, Mayor of London said: "The cost of Brexit crisis can only be solved if we take a mature approach". So we're screwed then.

A poll asked the question: From a list of professions, can you say whether you trust them to tell the truth or not.

Politicians were named the most trustworthy.

I'm lying, they came last. Professions deemed more trustworthy included football referees, lawyers, bankers, estate agents and "the ordinary man/woman in the street".

Our elected representatives are thought of as less trustworthy than any random person you might see waiting at a bus stop.

That's the Boris Effect.

Down to earth man of the people, Prime Minister Titchy Suitsize announced he was slapping a tax on flights within the UK. That is, the tax would apply to us, the little people, not to those such as himself who prefer to fly by helicopter and private jet. In fact, chopper fans won't pay a penny of tax, as it only applies to fixed wing aircraft.

Which was handy, if you were a Prime Minister positively addicted to travelling by helicopter at other people's expense.

To take the public's eye off this, he said "Stop the boats" a lot, without doing anything to actually stop the boats.

In IT news, Mark Zuckerberg, the moon-faced creep who runs Facebook, was accused of taking an irresponsible approach to artificial intelligence after committing to building an AI system on a par with human levels of intelligence.

This was nothing to be frightened about.

Human females on a night out wear shoes that are so uncomfortable they have to carry another pair of shoes to walk home in, and human males think darts is a sport.

Wouldn't it have been more responsible to aim a little ABOVE the level of human intelligence?

In a related development, the delivery firm DPD disabled part of its artificial intelligence powered online chatbot after it swore at a customer. It was happening – robots really were taking human's jobs.

In a parallel universe, where things work as they should, our water companies would be told to urgently tackle the sewage pollution crisis by a government demanding they clean up their act straight away.

We'll get on to that right now, the water companies would say, and the problem would be solved.

In our universe, if you went down to the sea, you were in for a brown surprise.

Meanwhile, the UK was found to be the "sick man" of Europe again. On almost every health indicator – life expectancy, healthy life expectancy, obesity rates and healthcare capacity – we lag behind our peers.

Something in the water?

February

As Barcelona residents were told that they couldn't fill their pools or wash their cars because of an ongoing drought, people in Britain were told that we were having the worst winter for storms on record, as in ever.

The government responded by granting 24 new licences to drill for fossil fuels in the North Sea.

Coincidentally, one of the Tory party's biggest donors was given one of those licences,. Funny how that kind of thing keeps happening. You simply donate a relatively small amount to the Conservative Party, and more often than not, you receive a relatively large amount of money back.

Best. Investment. Ever.

No-one paid any attention to that, however, because the produce on our supermarket shelves started appearing with the legend "Not for EU" stamped on them. This made everyone nervous about what it was that we were being fed that Europeans were rejecting.

Or at least that's what woke lefty surrender monkeys were thinking. True blue patriotic Brits were confident that the European Union would be jealous of our exclusive dinners, even if they were more expensive and filled with a noxious cocktail of harmful chemicals, just as Jacob Mee-Smugg promised, when he said that Brexit would deliver us cheaper food of greater quality.

Speaking of which, the government produced its Brexit Fourth Anniversary Update, which was filled with about as many true facts as a story beginning "Once upon a time..."

Kemi Bad Enoch found a way to insert a picture of herself on 10% of its pages.

In environment news, water company bosses and the heads of the body that is supposed to regulate them went for dinner at a private members club.

They met to discuss how water company bosses would forgo their bonuses to invest in their infrastructure. Just kidding, they met to discuss how to manage the public's anger about all the sewage we were swimming in, both literally and metaphorically.

The venue was one of those Pall Mall clubs that wouldn't let the likes of you or me in if we crawled up the steps and begged.

The menu included fish pie. Water company bosses did not order that, as they knew what fish had been swimming in.

Tory MP Flick Drummond advised that we should not flush the loo, take baths or use washing machines when it was raining to avoid sewage overflows into our rivers and seas. I am not making that up. Perhaps you had forgotten that the sewage in our waterways was our fault for acting as though we lived in a first world country, rather than the fault of the companies who had been making a mint by running the industry for the past 35 years.

It was Margaret Thatcher who sold our water off for nothing. She did the same to pretty much everything else we used to think of as ours and now is owned by the sort of international hedge fund and wealth management types that are the donor class.

But what do you sell when you have run down local councils over 14 years of Tory rule and they can't afford to empty our bins? Why, the buildings the councils are working from.

When you've sold everything in the cupboard, sell the cupboard.

This was the message from Michael Gove's Department for Levelling Up, which was a pretty funny name for a department that seemed to doing its best to level down everywhere that someone like Michael Gove would never go.

Channel 4 News reported on the state of the NHS and asked: How much better or worse was the NHS in England in 2023 compared to 2011?

They found that it was 10 times worse for 4-hour waits in A&E, 13 times worse for accessing care within 18 weeks, 14 times worse for waits for cancer treatment and 3,000 times worse for being kept on a trolley for 12 or more hours.

The Daily Mail tried to think how this could be Meghan Markle's fault.

In America, a Christian writer and editor in chief of Christianity Today said that some members of his faith were so enamoured of Donald Trump that they said that Jesus was weak by comparison. All that "turn the other cheek stuff" was just lefty liberal talking points to them.

"I hope those who've come to believe Trump is here to save us wake up before it's too late for us all," he said.

Spoiler alert: they didn't.

In Britain, a ban on XL bully dogs was brought in and made absolutely no difference to the number of those things dragging their tattooed gormless owners around and no difference to the number of attacks they launched.

The owners protested at the ban in scenes that looked like a prison yard social. But they love kids, they said, which is true. They find them delicious.

Man of the people Tetchy Sunak was wheeled into a dentists office by his handlers to promote the government's recovery plan for NHS dentistry.

He was photographed trying to appear normal in the company of normal people.

It might have gone better if the dental practice that was selected for him had not previously closed its books to the NHS and was seeing only private patients.

ITV News reported that things were so bad that some people had resorted to pulling their own teeth out.

Tory MP Victoria Atkins announced that if you find yourself in pain, you could always go the your local A&E, which would be excellent advice, except that A&E doesn't do dentistry.

She was the Health Secretary at the time. We're all lucky to be alive.

The UK economy was said to be 5 percent smaller than it would have been had we not voted for Brexit, stated the woke lefty communists at Goldman Sachs.

They issued a report that said, "The UK has notably lagged behind other developed economies since the 2016 EU referendum, experiencing slower growth and higher inflation".

Freedom!

Due to all of the above, the Conservatives were in a slump, so they came up with a new phrase they imagined would re-light the fire of our affection. We were encouraged to vote Conservative in the forthcoming election, or "go back to square one" with Labour.

Those with a long enough memory recalled that, on square one we could get our teeth seen to on the NHS, we didn't have to wait three weeks to see our GP, we had pay rises, there were libraries, we could afford our rent, we could buy stuff from Europe without import duties and endless red tape, the police would show up if we needed them, there were no queues at the borders, we could protest without fear of being thrown in jail and we could swim in the sea and rivers without needing to go to hospiotal afterwards.

Threatening us with square one under Labour was like threatening us with pudding. Yes please.

In transport news, railway companies had long been criticised for making tickets too complicated. In order to bring clarity to buying tickets, "simpler fares" were introduced.

These simply made journeys from London to Edinburgh, for instance, more than double in price. Super off-peak fares of £87 were replaced with simple "anytime" fares that cost £193 each way. Problem solved.

Happily and coincidentally, the private firms that lease out trains for Britain's railway had seen their profits treble in a year.

Run for the benefit of their shareholders and executives, they had paid out more than £400m in dividends in one year

It was pretty much the only thing about the trains that runs reliably on time - pay day for the owners.

Labour won the Wellingborough by-election, securing a 28.5 percentage-point swing from the Conservatives, in the biggest Labour victory over the Tories since 1994 and the second biggest since the war.

The party had made six by-election gains since 2019.

The Conservatives had lost 10 by-elections in that time. Was it something they did?

Titchi Suitsize encouraged us to "stick to the plan because the plan is working".

He also said the word "priorities" a lot, as though his and ours were somehow connected.

In America, Donald Trump and his family business were fined $364 million in a New York civil fraud trial. It followed a three-month court case in which Trump, to obtain favourable terms on loans from banks, was accused of massively inflating the values of his properties, including Mar-a-Lago and a Trump Tower penthouse.

Trump was magnanimous in defeat and vowed to run his affairs more ethically in future.

And if you believe that, I have a non-fungible token of Trump drawn as a superhero I would like to sell you.

Weather-wise it was such an unlovey day, when torrential rain caused flooded roads, blocked rail lines, buses were cancelled and schools closed in Shropshire, Worcestershire, Herefordshire and

Warwickshire. Basically, anywhere that ends in "shire".

People were rescued from stranded cars on deluged roads, whole towns were washed out to sea, there were hailstones so big they could knock out a moose, we had sewage up to our nostrils and the usual things that happen whenever it rains in Great Britain.

All perfectly normal in a well-run country.

Germany joined the list of nations that had legalised cannabis for personal use. They announced that the law would come into being on April 1st, which was not a joke.

In this country, our politicians still thought that the best course of action was to stick to the War on Drugs, a policy that had failed every year for 60 years in every country in which it had been tried, because, you know, that'll work.

In case you only recall farmers protesting about inheritance tax that they probably won't pay anyway, a reminder that they were protesting a lot before Labour got a sniff of power.

Farmers' protests had been sweeping Europe for months.

In Greece, the country's farmers were angry that the government hadn't honoured a promise to compensate them for income lost following a period of ruinous weather.

In Germany, farmers took to the streets after the government unveiled plans to phase out a tax break on agricultural diesel. Portugal, Poland and France had also been hit by demonstrations.

Meanwhile, British farmers angrily protested at cheap food imports, and the rotten post-Brexit deal that was imposed on them by the Tory government. They drove over Westminster Bridge on tractors daubed with signs saying "No farmers, no food", which they managed to recycle later on in the year, when they demanded a return of the Tory government they were complaining about.

Meanwhile, Liz "The Blunder" Truss sparked speculation that she was eyeing a political comeback.

The voices in her head had convinced her that she was very popular with the public, despite all the evidence to the contrary.

She urged Nigel Farage to join the Tories and "help turn our country around" and stated that her premiership would have succeeded were it not for the lefty wokerati of the financial community.

At one of those right-wing think-ins in America, she decried those who are Chinos, or "Conservatives in name only".

Liz Truss said that Chinos are, "people who think, I want to be popular, I don't want to upset people, I don't want to look like a mean person, I want to attend nice dinner parties in London or Washington DC, I want my friends to like me, I don't want to cause trouble"

Imagine the inside of the persons mind who thinks that any of that is bad.

So, her preference would be to be unpopular, to upset people, to look like a mean person, not get invited to dinner and wanted her friends to not like her and to cause trouble.

Well, good news Liz...

In corruption news, under legislation to crack down on fraud, the number of cases opened by a HM Revenue and Customs unit investigating the donor class of offshore, corporate and wealthy taxpayers fell by more than half in five years.

Isn't that totally surprising?

Also not entirely shocking was the failed launch of a nuclear capable missile from a British submarine off the coast of Florida. This was the second time such a thing had failed in eight years.

The missiles were supposed to be able to travel more than 4,000 miles but we would be lucky if they managed to clear the submarine they're fired from before they explode.

Still, its not like there were any wars on or anything.

March

Chile and Australia were suffering forest fires, South Africa was experiencing record heat waves, Madagascar faced food shortages linked to climate change and February was declared to have been the hottest on record in the UK. But no body cared about that because...

The things that used to be ours had been flogged off to foreign investors and now that they had our fuel, transport and water, they were after our companies too. The entire country had a For Sale sign up. Everything was going cheap in UK plc.

Get 'em quick. You won't believe these prices!

Businesses you thought were British had either already been absorbed into foreign companies or were about to be carved up and sold off.

This included the firm that prints our money. We don't get our passports made in this country any more and it looked like the only thing left in British ownership would be Wetherspoons, in which we could contemplate the sun setting on this once great nation with some Dutch, German, American, Japanese or Australian beer.

George Galloway won the Rochdale by-election. This was reported on like it was the end of the world, as though that was it for the democratic process and catastrophe beckoned.

And then nothing happened. We got to see him without his hat, when he appeared in the Commons and that was about it.

Some of the good people of Rochdale were furious about him winning, but the turnout was less than 40%, so they got what they couldn't be bothered not to vote for.

The cat in the hat returned to Westminster after a nine-year absence as a representative of a third different political party - the Workers Party of Britain - having previously been both a Labour and Respect MP.

He had loyally served three political parties and four wives.

The man must have been exhausted.

The Tories suspended Lee Anderson for saying something calculatedly stupid about the London Mayor Sadiq Khan.

Richard Tice of Farage's Reform had reportedly been in talks with Nee Anderthall to join the Nigel cult. Tice had previously claimed he had rejected two Tory MPs trying to defect to Reform as they did not share the party's "values, principles and integrity".

He actually did say that.

Chancellor Jeremy Hunt and Rishi Sunak were forced to tear up their proposed Budget at the last minute after the Office for Budget Responsibility told them it was unaffordable.

They wanted sweets AND comics but nanny said they could have only one.

The mood of the nation had turned against them, though.

The public had finally got to the place where it wouldn't get fooled by promises of rainbows and unicorns any more.

They could say that they'd give each and every one if us a cheque for a billion pounds and personal foot massage if they wanted, no one believed them any more.

How does the phrase go? Fool us once, shame on them. Fool us over and over again, we're morons.

Something like that.

Tory grandees were furious. Jacob Mee-Smugg, melting waxwork David Frost and John 'Deadwood' Redwood urged the government to ignore the OBR.

Great advice, because the last time a Prime Minister did that under the catastrophic exploding premiership of The Blundertruss, it went really well.

Days before the budget, wealthy Tory donors paid £25,000 for a cosy private dinner with the Chancellor. A Conservative Part fundraiser in one of London's fancier hotels saw items auctioned including a picture of the Cabinet which made £115,000.

For a picture. Of the Cabinet.

Tetchy Sunak, Home Secretary James Cleverly, Foreign Secretary David Cameron and Defence Secretary Grant Shapps all attended the party, arriving by government limousine despite their offices being around five minutes walk away.

We were paying for them to go there, so they could get fed and make money for themselves. What sounds crooked about that?

The meal itself was a modest affair.

Starters of rainbow trout with a squid ink emulsion and babies, or Yorkshire celeriac with vegetarians.

A main course of Hereford beef fillet and oxtail, served with creamed slaves, with herb crusted King Oyster mushrooms and fondant plebeians.

The vegan option was, "get out you woke lefty".

Back in Westminster, Business Secretary Kemi BadEnoch insisted that the UK was succeeding on the world stage by "embracing free trade".

We appeared to be doing that by erecting trade barriers between us and our biggest market.

She also said that the country was thriving outside the EU.

In the real world, growth had fallen for two quarters in a row, the EU had beaten us in economic performance in each of the past four quarters. Our GDP had risen by 1% since the pandemic, while the EU had done three times as well. But sure, "thriving".

In health news, the Health Secretary was Victoria Atkins, and as if that wasn't scary enough, she was proposing that artificial intelligence robots should sit in on GP appointments.

We could look forward to seeing our doctor while a robot would automatically generate notes in the background, and presumably do a costing of your treatment and suggest alternatives, like being placed on a iceberg and getting pushed out to sea.

In order to demonstrate the precision of the technology, Victoria Atkins had a robot transcribe her speech as she announced the plan.

It mistook her mention of the chief medical officer Chris Whitty, writing it as "Christmas".

Christmas had approved the plan. Santa was on board.

In rock news, The Sex Pistols' John Lydon claimed people arriving into Britain were creating animosity in communities, and that the country today is "so, so catastrophically disappointing".

Hey Johnny, you know what else is so, so catastrophically disappointing?

Starts with a J.

He said "A lot of this tour that I'm doing will be in seaside towns and they really indicate how run down Britain has become. They used to be fantastic places when I was a kid. Mum and dad would drag us off there for what felt like hours in a traffic jam. But it was absolutely great. It was working class people throwing sand at each other."

Funny how things that happened in your youth are great in the rear view mirror, because your knees worked , and you had the benefit of not expecting too much.

Seaside towns had been in a downward spiral since the 1960s, since it became cheaper to fly to sunny Spain for a holiday than to go to rainy Rhyl.

Could this be the same Johnny Rotten that sang about God save the Queen, the fascist regime?

The butter seller's new tour was called "I could be wrong, I could be right".

Wrong, then.

The budget was delivered and it was found that pensioners were the "biggest losers" from the Budget – taking an £8billion collective hit.

The Institute for Fiscal Studies (IFS) and the Resolution Foundation said stealth taxes would leave the elderly poorer at the end of this Parliament and that most pensioners will be £650-a-year worse off by 2027 while higher-rate taxpayer pensioners will be more than £3,000-a-year worse off.

Absolutely everyone would forget that the moment Labour came to power later in the year.

Setting a great example for the kids, Gillian Keegan the Secretary of State for Education of the United Kingdom told a headteacher's conference that she would "have probably punched" Ofsted inspectors, based on an account she had heard during a recent school visit.

She's the one that complained about not being praised enough for doing a "f***ing good job" when she was found to be presiding over the aerated concrete issue of schools actually collapsing and children having to be taught in Portakabins for fear they might get crushed under tons of rubble. She also declared that children actually prefer to be taught in a cabin!

This was the same Gillian Keegan who flashed a £10,000 Rolex watch on her wrist while telling teachers to reign in their pay demands. She also claimed that teachers were "probably in the top 10 per cent of earners in some parts of the country".

Extra maths homework for Gillian. Could try harder.

In transport news, Prime Minister Fishi Sunak personally intervened to stop the scrapping of VIP helicopters for his own use.

In 2023, Ben Wallace, the former defence secretary, ended a contract for two private helicopters used by politicians. The contract was due to come to a close at the end of September. Sunak stopped that stopping.

In order to connect with the British people, he would shun the train and instead waft about in a private cloud of padded loveliness.

The £40m bill would be picked up by us poor dopes he would be flying over.

MPs, many of whom were furious at teachers and doctors asking for a pay rise, were delighted to learn that MPs would be getting a pay rise. All of their arguments against raising the wages of the people who teach and care for us did not apply to their own circumstance, and they welcomed the 5.5% hike to £91,000 a year, plus £250,000 expenses.

Fun fact: MPs' wages had increased by 39% since 2010, compared to just 8% for the average Brit.

If a typical voter in 2010 had achieved the same rate of pay increase over the last 14 years, they'd have an extra £8,000 a year in their pay packet.

MPs were worth it. We weren't.

Liz Truss went on a £20,000 trip paid for by a mysterious political organisation to attend a secretive meeting on a privately-owned island.

What sounds odd about that?

The former Prime Minister and South West Norfolk MP travelled to Sea Island, off the coast of Georgia in the US, for an event described as a "small gathering of the great minds of today".

Or it might have been a "great gathering of the small minds of today".

Meanwhile, back in Westminster, a Tory exodus was gathering pace.

Defence minister James Heappey quit amid a row over funding saying he wanted to 'prioritise family' and 'pursue a different career'.

Which begged the question, who's James Heappey?

He was the 62nd Tory MP over the past week to announce he was stepping down, including ex-PM Theresa May, who would not so much step down as totter down in shoes she could barely walk in.

What did Drear Leader Tetchi say about this?

As he was buying goodbye cards in bulk and there were more leaving do's than there were hours in the day, he said that the Tories were "united".

The poor man was under a lot of pressure, so maybe he wasn't thinking straight.

There was the row over donations from a millionaire Tory donor who allegedly said Diane Abbott "should be shot".

The Prime Minister resisted calls to hand back £15 million in donations from Frank Hester, a party backer who was alleged to have said that Diane Abbott, Britain's first black female MP, made him want to hate all black women and that she should be shot, in comments the Prime Minister described as "racist" after initially refusing to do so.

He could not countenance returning the money, however, citing 15 million reasons why not.

Lee Anderthall, ex-Tory Party deputy chairman and newly defected member of Farage's Reform took a triumphant open top bus tour of his Nottinghamshire seat.

Press pictures captured the scene as he paraded down empty streets in what he calls "the capital of common sense".

He said, "This a typical red wall area. This is where people speak plain English and are not afraid to speak plain English."

He's right. Almost no one showed up save for a nice lady that called him a w***er", in plain English.

In other unpleasantness, we were warned of possible outbreaks of disease across the UK following incidences of sewage spilling into gardens and city streets, in scenes not seen since Victorian times.

The phenomenon known as "sewer flooding", saw untreated contents of the pipes spill out onto roads and gardens.

Some told how sewage had leaked onto their properties after just moderate rainfall, with poop, toilet paper and other unprocessed waste visibly floating on top.

The Tories under Thatcher had gifted corporations and wealth funds monopoly ownership of the most essential thing to life, and since these lucky people got control over our water industry, instead of fixing its many problems, they had instead given themselves £60bn in dividends for excellence in being themselves.

Nobody cared about that, however, because the nation was gripped with fury about a change to a small flag on the England football team shirt.

Fishi slammed Nike and the Football Association for changing the colours of the St George's Cross on the new England shirt, insisting: "When it comes to our national flags, we shouldn't mess with them".

He was the leader of the same Conservative Party that had displayed the Union Flag morphed into the shape of a tree and rendered all in blue as their logo at the 2019 Tory leadership election.

There was raw sewage pouring into our rivers, pot holes in the roads you could lose you car in, social care was non existent in large parts of the country, the NHS had been dismantled to the extent that what was the envy of the world 14 years ago now saw people go to other countries to get treated rather than wait on a list for treatment so long they'd likely be dead before they get better. Councils couldn't cope with the underfunding they'd suffered by central government, you couldn't rely on the police any more, children were going to bed hungry, schools were in danger of falling down, we were trailing behind the rest of the world because of the disaster that was Brexit and since they had come to power the Tories had borrowed half a trillion pounds before Covid and another half a trillion since, and no one could think of a thing they had done with it that benefitted us poor dopes who pay taxes.

And what were our governing party obsessed about?

The colour on a shirt they wouldn't buy for a game they don't watch because rugby's more their thing.

In other patriotic news, the Victoria and Albert museum staged a display of the history of comedy and described Margaret Thatcher as "an unpopular figure".

The purple faced fury brigade had a fit you could see from the International Space Station.

A display case devoted to Punch and Judy sported a caption which read, "Over the years, the evil character in this seaside puppet show has shifted from the Devil to unpopular public figures including Adolf Hitler, Margaret Thatcher and Osama bin Laden, to offer contemporary villains."

After enough ink to paint the Forth Bridge was used to express the anger of the right wing newspapers and their permanently enraged readership, the V&A changed it to read, "The characters have since been re-cast to reflect figures in the public eye – from Adolf Hitler during wartime to Margaret Thatcher in the 1980s being portrayed as villains, to more recently Nick Clegg as the clown and Simon Cowell as the judge."

Tory grandee Sir Iain Duncan Smith continued to be un-amused: "They must live in a bubble, away from the real world to think that it is rational to propose that a politician of the stature of Margaret Thatcher would equate to any of those mass murderers and vile human beings. This sort of idiocy begs the question about government funding", he said.

And it does. This sort of idiocy begs the question: should we de-fund the government?

In scenes that would be forgotten when Labour came to power, farmers drove dozens of tractors in a slow-motion convoy towards Parliament to protest post- Brexit rules and trade deals that they say are endangering livelihoods and food security.

A line of tractors flying Union Jack flags or signs reading "Stop substandard imports" snaked along the River Thames and towards the Houses of Parliament before circling Parliament Square to cheers and honking horns.

Jeremy Clarkson was nowhere to be seen, so it didn't really make the news.

In sport, the Oxford and Cambridge Boat Race took place.

Oxford team captain Lenny Jenkins blamed E.coli in the water for their defeat against Cambridge, saying he was vomiting before the start of the race.

He said there was too much poop in the water, which begs the question, how much is too much?

April

The month began with two storms in two days

Storms Olivia and Katherine hit, only one of which would have caused the usual cancellations, closures and chaos.

Both together was a disaster, but no one was bothered with that because...

A Tory minister declared that the UK government should appoint a Minister for Flags.

I am not making that up.

This was a further development in the confected row about the Cross of St George on the England football team's shirts.

Nike had altered the English flag, introducing purple and blue horizontal stripes in what it called a "playful update" to the team shirt ahead of Euro 2024.

In the minds of the fury brigade, "playful update" translated as "gay" and they took to the airwaves and papers to hyperventilate about this being one woke step too far.

They were making a stand for the sanctity of the flag, standing in front of their own Conservative and Reform party flags that had been playfully updated by their own design teams to make brand logos out of an altered Union Jack.

Reform's was a sliver of the flag with their own logo in the middle. The Tories had changed it into a tree, for some reason.

If they had turned round, they would have seen what giant asses they were making of themselves, but they were not for turning, as their hair-sprayed heroine once memorably said.

It was either richly ironic, or dismally depressing, that the Conservative MP Esther McVey, the "Minister for Common Sense", made the biggest noise about this.

In less important news, the government was rolling out the use of Physicians' Associates in GP practices across the land.

This was to address the lack of GPs and the time it took to gain an appointment with one.

Now, with Physicians' Associates you would be seen more quickly, but by a person that was not qualified as an actual doctor.

Problem solved.

The government assured nervous patients that those PA's would have a science background, then undid their case by confirming that someone with a science background would include those with a degree in geography.

"Can you point to where on this map you are feeling the pain?"

To avoid being seen by a non-doctor, you would have to go private, but most people didn't have the money because the energy giants had taken it all.

Together, they had made £420 billion profit in the past four years. Those were the years of sky-high fuel bills that coincided with the Ukraine war and the hang-over from Covid.

They didn't look a gift crisis in the mouth

In other money news, the Chancellor Jeremy Hunt's budget addressed the status of non-doms who use the rules to avoid the level of taxes that us little people were subject to.

Analysis of the policy announced by Hunt saw it riddled with loopholes that someone like Prime Minister Rishi Sunak could benefit from, to the tune of £250 million in savings on his family's tax bill per year.

Every little helps.

Looking forward to the election, Labour announced plans to restrict MPs second jobs. They suggested that a Labour government would ban a serving MP from holding second, third, fourth and fifth jobs, so that they might concentrate on doing their actual job of being a Member of Parliament.

It was to be a total ban, except for giving paid speeches and broadcast work. So, not so much a ban then, as not a ban.

Some MPs were earning more from outside work than the generous amount, plus expenses, that they were being paid for doing the job they were elected to do, which made us wonder whether being an MP was really their second job.

To take our minds off all that, the Tories released an advert with the slogan "Don't talk our country down", aimed squarely at Labour.

"Britain is the second most powerful country in the world", it said with a collage that featured the less than powerful looking Titchi Suitsize as its biggest image.

The ad included pictures of King Charles in a sparkly hat, encrusted with jewels we stole from the Third World, images of an F-35, which was a US fighter jet, the Eurofighter from the European Union, our unelected Prime Minister born to Indian and African parents, The England football team, which doesn't represent Britain, a cargo ship registered in Panama, an Aston Martin, the main shareholders of which are led by a Canadian billionaire and which use German engines, and the film director Christopher Nolan, who lives in America.

Other than that, it was as British as it could be.

While the Conservatives were celebrating British Britishness, the UK was voted the second most miserable place in the world.

Only Uzbekistan ranked lower than the UK in a global mental wellbeing index.

The Sapien Labs' Mental State of the Year report took results from 500,000 respondents, from 71 countries, then compared countries by giving them a score.

On a scale of zero to 200, where zero is Hell and 200 is Heaven, Britain scored a pitiful 49, while the average among all countries was 65.

Anything less than 50 was classed as "enduring"

Britons were enduring - just suffering through life.

If the government had spent a little less time creating risible collages in a desperate attempt to cling on to the power they didn't deserve, and a little more time trying to make things better for us poor dopes who pay taxes, then we might actually *feel* like we were the second most powerful country in the world, apart from Germany that is, and France, Japan, China and India and, by the time you are reading this, probably Narnia too.

In "taxes are for little people" news, Starbucks were found to have paid £7.2 million in UK corporation tax on a profit of £149 million in the previous year.

Starbucks Coffee Company (UK) made a £149m "gross profit" in the year to October 2023, but after "administrative expenses" of £127m, its pre-tax profits were reduced to £16.9m, on which it paid £7.2m tax.

In related news, Starbucks EMEA, which collects royalty payments from the UK and 42 countries across Europe, the Middle East and Africa paid a $325m (£257m) dividend to the coffee chain's parent company in Seattle.

That's a lot of administration.

That's a taxation rate of 4.8%. Don't try and pay 4.8% tax on your income, as things might go as well for you as for the executives of the coffee chain.

Duncan Moir, the president of Starbucks EMEA, said: "We are pleased to report another strong year of revenue growth, owing in large part to the dedication, hard work and relentless pursuit of excellence that our brilliant team of accountants and lawyers continue to deliver."

He did not say that, I made that up. He really said "We are pleased to report another strong year of revenue growth, owing in large part to the dedication, hard work and relentless pursuit of excellence that our brilliant team of partners continue to deliver."

I think by "partners", he means those low wage people who press a button that makes water pour through ground beans and who call themselves baristas.

Cost of living update: UK insurers revealed the amount they paid out for motor claims went up by about 18% last year, but British drivers faced premium increases of more than a third

As you would expect, the cost of insurance in this country is much higher than the same thing in Europe because...you know...freedom.

The Association of British Insurers (ABI) put the average increase for car cover in the UK at 34%, with many drivers having seen a doubling of their previous year's bill.

In Europe by contrast, car premiums over the same period rose by 6% in Italy, 5% in Spain and 2% in France.

We were being taken for a ride...in our own cars!

Meanwhile, the Doomsday Clock was reading 90 seconds to midnight. Endless articles explaining how we were all going to die covered acres of space in our national newspapers, who tried to make this somehow Meghan Markles' fault.

We were told that if Russia attacked London with a missile on Westminster, the radiation would reach Chelsea, but as nobody actually lives in Chelsea and the houses there were bought with Roubles as safe investments, it seems unlikely that Vlad would bomb his own money.

He might bomb Yorkshire though, which is where Fishi Sunak had a home. To reassure us that he would be OK, the Prime Minister said that his cashmere lined bomb shelter and swimming pool complex was working perfectly and would be maintained at a comfortable 20 degrees centigrade, while residents outside would bask in a billion degree heatwave.

In what was perfectly normal in Toryland, William Wragg, chairman of a Commons select committee, told The Times he handed over the personal phone numbers of colleagues to a man he met on Grindr, a gay dating app.

Wragg, the vice-chairman of the 1922 Committee, said he provided the details after sending intimate pictures of himself to the user.

Wragg said he was "scared" that the man "had compromising things on me".

He was being manipulated, and not in a good way.

Those colleagues — which included several MPs, members of their staff and a political journalist — were subsequently sent unsolicited flirtatious messages from people identifying themselves as "Charlie" or "Abi" who said that they had met the MPs being targetted when they used to work in one of the parliamentary bars and bragged about having sex with several Conservative MPs.

I'm not sure that "bragged " is the correct word here, "confessed" would be nearer the mark.

The messages from "Charlie" or "Abi" quickly moved to the exchange of explicit pictures and at least three MPs responded in kind

We were not really dealing with the brightest bulbs here.

Fun fact: William Wragg was a member of the Conservative Common Sense Group!

The Post Office scandal rumbled on, after the TV drama "Mr Bates vs the Post Office" had forced ministers to address the issue they had spent the previous two decades ignoring.

Nothing like a bit of prime time television guilt-tripping to focus the mind.

Software from Fujitsu was in the firing line, so naturally, the government thought it would be a good idea to announce they had given the contract for software support for the National Nuclear Laboratory to the very same Fujitsu, because after all, what could possibly go wrong?

Happily, the nation was buoyed by the news that His Majesty King Charles III was to receive a 45% increase in his remuneration for all that exhausting waving he does.

The Sovereign Grant was to be increased from a mere £86m per year to a much more appropriate £125m, because he's worth it.

Meanwhile, outside the royal palaces, houses, cottages, castles, manors, estates, mansions and halls, His Majesty's subjects gratefully went to bed hungry and cold, glad to be suffering so that he didn't have to.

In politics, with the election nearing, the various forms of ID that would be needed to cast your vote were listed. These included everything that an old person might possess and nothing that a young person would have.

For instance, an old person's bus pass was just fine, a young person's bus pass was not.

The fact that the young tend not to vote Conservative was a total coincidence.

Team GB launched the official Adidas Olympic kit. After Nike had been savaged by the purple faced fury-mongers for messing with the cross of St George on the England strip, Adidas seemed to forgo the flag altogether and just plastered "Great Britain" in pink on a plain blue background.

After blasting the Nike "playful" update for being too playful, the press blasted the Adidas effort for not being playful enough.

It was "basic and unimaginative" wailed the usual suspects. Is there anything they won't complain about?

In poop news, a whistleblower revealed that water companies were diverting sewage directly into rivers and seashores because if they just got rid of it that way, they could say that they were treating a greater proportion of the sewage that came into their works, because they were getting less of it.

They could boast that their sewage works remained spotlessly clean, while surrounded by lakes of the excrement. One insider said that about a third of the sewage they were supposed to be cleaning went straight into the environment because then they didn't have to deal with it.

Problem solved.

The regulator Ofwat said water companies' environmental performance was "simply not good enough", as though they were not the very people who were supposed to prevent this from happening.

Chris Philp was the Policing Minister and appeared on TV's Question Time and was asked whether people from Congo who are at war with Rwanda would be sent to Rwanda if they managed to make it here.

Philp wondered aloud whether Congo was a separate country to Rwanda.

He also questioned whether East Africa was near West Africa, and if so, wasn't that a bit of a coincidence, and also wondered if Tanzania is in Australia and how to pronounce N-I-G-E-R.

I made some of that up, but not all of it.

The minister said: "Well Rwanda is a different country from Congo, isn't it?" His response sparked laughter and mockery, mostly from people who couldn't pinpoint Rwanda on a map if their lives depended on it.

Philp is a Tiggerish sort and his willingness to spout the party line on absolutely anything at all meant he was seldom off our screens.

He was asked how he would score the Liz Truss Special Operations Budget and he gave it a 9.5 out of 10.

Do you need to know anything more about him?

In crime news, the government announced that assaulting a shop worker would be made a separate criminal offence in England and Wales in response to a wave of retail crime.

Earlier this year a report found violent and abusive incidents against shop workers rose by 50% in 2022-23.

Rishi Sunak said shops must be free from the threat of crime or abuse.

If only the party of law and order, the Conservative Party, had been in power this past 14 years, they might have been in a position to do something about it, but sadly we had been run by the communist regime of Jeremy Corbyn.

Thanks a lot Jeremy Corby, see what you've done?

The new offence of attacking shop workers would carry a maximum sentence of six months, as opposed to the current law about attacking shop workers which carried a maximum sentence of the very same six months.

However, anyone convicted of the new offence would not routinely go to prison.
The Sentencing Bill would mean sentences of 12 months or less would be suspended

So this new law was coming over all tough while being as empty as the supermarket shelf they used to keep the razor blades on.

A Norwegian newspaper wrote an article about what it is like to live in Britain. It was not complimentary.

They wrote about being overwhelmed by bad news from the moment they arrived in the country, about homelessness doubling, schools crumbling, infant mortality rising, hospital waiting lists increasing, political scandals multiplying, food banks proliferating all amounting to a "mosaic of decay" that reads like a crime novel.

As a sort of killer blow, a former Danish finance minister noted that, "There are two types of nations in Europe. Small nations and countries that have not yet realized that they are small nations."

Ouch!

In better news, the Tory candidate for mayor of London, Susan Hall, announced her keystone policy for the Capital: banning people taking calls on speaker-phone on the Tube.
Take that Norway!

Elsewhere in Toryland, top minister James Cleverly made a joke about Fishi Sunak's height.

This may come as a surprise to those with short memories, but Cleverly was the Home Secretary for a brief period. Recounting the time when he was moved from the Foreign Office to the Home Office, he said that during talks in No10, the PM "looked him in the eye", but "had to stand on his wallet to do so."

Funny, no?

Meanwhile, Foreign Secretary David Cameron departed on a whistle-stop tour of Asia.

It was the first high-level visit to Mongolia by a UK minister in a decade.

The peer had also been to Tajikistan, Kyrgyzstan, Uzbekistan, Turkmenistan and Kazakhstan. Basically, all the Stans.

Cameron announced £50million of development funding for the region over the next three years, which struck many as an insultingly small amount of money to offer the government of one whole country, never mind a handful of them.

In return we could have our fill of yaks milk, or whatever it is that the Stans specialise in.

Hopefully his Lordship was able to fit in a little personal business while he was there, in amongst all the selfless service.

In bad news for the administration, Conservative MP Dan Poulter defected to Labour.

The ex-health minister and part time as a doctor, said he found it 'increasingly difficult to look his NHS colleagues in the eye' while being a Tory.

He could have borrowed Fishi's wallet to stand on.

He claimed the Conservatives were not prioritising public services, saying they no longer had a "compassionate view about supporting the more disadvantaged in society".

He had apparently just come to that conclusion.

Perhaps he had been under general anaesthetic for the past 14 years, because that's how long he had been a Tory MP, and he had only just noticed that they lack compassion.

He said, "It's time to end the Conservative chaos, turn the page and get Britain's future back", parroting the nonsense phrase the Labour Party had adopted in order to appeal to those members of the public who can only think in pithy slogans.

"Let's get Britain's future back" was so bad on so many levels.

It was clumsy, more than the regulation three words and it didn't even make sense.

It was an attempt at Trumpification but was too long to fit on a hat.

Labour weren't really very good at this sort of thing, but fortunately for them, the Tories were even worse.

May

After heavy storms slammed the region, the Houston area was suffering flood conditions and authorities warned those in low-lying areas to evacuate.

For weeks, drenching rains in Texas and parts of Louisiana had filled reservoirs and saturated the ground. Flood waters submerged cars and waters reached the roofs of some homes.

Then, more than 11in (28cm) of rain fell during a 24-hour period.

The US National Hurricane Center forecasters predicted one of the most active hurricane seasons on record, expecting double the number of huge storms that used to be the case ten years previously.

This was not anything to do with climate change though, according to people who don't believe in science.

The UK had been hit by 11 named storms since September, and experienced the wettest 18-month period since records began in 1836.

But no-one cared about that because...

Boris Johnson had said in 2004 that if the law ever required the production of ID to vote, he would eat his at a polling station in protest.
Turns out that was one of the many things he did not tell the truth about.

In 2022, he passed a law requiring ID to vote and dismissed criticism it would stop people voting.
Then, a year later that top-hatted twiglet Smugg admitted that it *had* stopped people voting in the local elections - the wrong people.
He said the elderly had forgotten to take their ID and that attempt by his own party to "gerrymander", or steal the elections, had backfired.
These people feel so immune to the consequences of their own actions they feel comfortable saying the quiet part out loud.

Then, in an un-stunning development, that could have been predicted by anyone who knows anything about the man, Mr Blobby was turned away from his local polling station when trying to vote in the local elections after forgetting to bring his own acceptable form of photo identification.

He used to run the country. We're lucky to be alive.

In answer to a demand that no-one had ever made, it was announced that pint-sized bottles of wine were set to appear on UK shelves from September due to new post-Brexit sovereignty.

No longer would we have to consume wine in European surrender measurements. We would be able to drink French wine in pints, because that is freedom, as anyone who has had a couple of pints of wine would tell you.

Business minister Kevin Hollinrake said changes to pre-packaged wine sizes were due to come into force on September 19, and insisted they would support the UK wine sector by providing opportunities for "innovation and greater choice".

Where did they get these people who were prepared to say this stuff in public?

There's already a 500ml bottle size, quite how there's a pent-up demand for a pint bottle, which is 568ml, is something known only to him.

The right-wing press were predicting that the race to be London mayor was going to result in the unseating of Sadiq Kahn and that Tory candidate Susan Hall was definitely on track to win.

She wasn't and didn't.

It emerged she had liked posts picturing Enoch Powell with the caption, "It's never too late to get London back!" and which referred to Khan as the "mayor of Londonistan" and said that Khan must be stopped from charging London's drivers by the mile.

Khan had always said he had no intention of doing that.

During her campaign, Hall admitted that she did not know the price of a bus fare, the starting salary of a police officer, or who controlled Hammersmith Bridge across the River Thames, which is at the heart of a bitter funding row.

She also could not point to London on a map, said she didn't like whelks or pie and mash and that maybe its because she's not a Londoner that she doesn't love old London town

She didn't say any of those things. I made them up. If she's allowed to make up stuff, why can't I?

In the U.S., it was discovered that IQ scores were dropping for the first time on record. The drop was especially pronounced in certain states. New Hampshire was the state with the smartest people, followed by Massachusetts, Minnesota and Vermont. The states with the lowest IQ were found to be Louisiana, Mississippi and Alabama.

If you need me to tell you which of those states vote Democrat and which vote Republican, then you probably live in Louisiana, Mississippi or Alabama.

The researchers tried to find a reason why intelligence levels were declining overall and pointed the finger at the computer in our pockets.

Our smart phones were making us stupid.

Britain's entry to the Eurovision Song Contest featured what one concerned paper described as "five half-naked men simulating sex acts in a grotty, neon-lit lavatory".

Olly Alexander represented Britain in a red codpiece, gyrating while licking his lips as his backing dancers rubbed each other's torsos and bounced around on all-fours.

Cliff Richard it was not. Neither was it winning.

To buoy the nation, Kier Starmer welcomed a new recruit to the team.

The Labour party should be "less tribal" and be open to "reasonably minded people, whichever way they voted in the past", Starmer said, welcoming Labour's newest MP, Natalie Elphicke, and was immediately forced to apologise for her comments about her husband's victims.

Charlie Elphicke was convicted of sexually assaulting two women and sentenced to two years in prison in 2020.

Natalie Elphicke supported his unsuccessful appeal, saying he was an "attractive" man who had been "an easy target for dirty politics and false allegations".

After her apology a member of Labour's ruling National Executive Committee called for her to be investigated and have the whip suspended, just 24 hours after she had joined the party.

Starmer insisted her defection from the Conservatives was proof that the Labour party was building a broad range of support.

True – they had kooks and crackpots and numpties and ne'r-do-wells, and some were good people, I suppose.

Meanwhile, Lord Blencathra, a Tory peer, demanded a total ban on cat flaps to protect birds from their hunting habits.

The ex-minister warned that cats allowed to roam freely were killing 60million garden birds a year.

This was the same Baron Blencathra who worked extensively with the pro-hunting group Vote-OK, with the aim of having the Hunting Act 2004 repealed, the act that banned hunting animals with dogs.

Cats hunting: bad; dogs hunting: good.

The difference is that toffs cant ride along with the cats on their hunt.

Lord Blencathra also said collars with bells should be compulsory for felines so they cannot sneak up on prey.

The same thing could be used on some Tory MPs, to keep their assistants safe from being sneaked up on by *them*.

In a puff piece about the UK's number one family, it was revealed that the Sunak's are a very down-to-earth lot and like nothing better than shopping at the local supermarket and taking the dog for a walk.

We learned that when the Sunaks travelled by train to his constituency in Richmond, North Yorkshire, they took their Tupperware stored leftovers with them.

Their frugality could also be seen in their choice of perfectly ordinary homes.

The Sunaks owned a £7 million town-house and a £1million flat in Kensington, as well as a £5.5million penthouse in California, overlooking Santa Monica pier, and the £2million mansion in Rishi's Yorkshire constituency, where he is nicknamed the 'Maharaja of the Dales'.

According to the latest edition of the Sunday Times Rich List, Fishi and his wife Akshata Murty added £120 million to their personal fortune over the past year, bringing their estimated combined wealth to £651 million.

Akshata Murty received about £11.5m a year in dividends from a stake in an Indian IT firm and had declared non-dom status, which allows people to avoid tax on foreign earnings.

Her spokesperson said all necessary tax was paid by Murty but declined to say where, as that information was not "relevant".

Which sounds very much like: don't question us peasant.

But please…do go on about your Tupperware leftovers.

In other money news, we found that King Charles' personal wealth had jumped by £10million to £610million in the last year, making him much richer than his mother Queen Elizabeth II who was worth a mere £370million.

His Kingness inherited private estates Sandringham in Norfolk and Balmoral in Aberdeenshire, passed to him directly without having to pay a penny in inheritance taxes.

Taxes are for the little people (not leprechauns).

Us poor dopes who actually do pay taxes were gifting him a 45% pay rise next year.

Hair oil and cufflinks aren't cheap, you know.

The respected Chandler Good Government Index was published for the year, in which Britain dropped out of the top 10 best-run countries.

Britain's place on the annual list was made worse by scores for "leadership and foresight" putting it in 20th place.

It was also hit by coming 27th in "financial stewardship", despite the fact that we were being run by a bloke whose fortune, outside of the one he married into, was made in finance.

He made £100m because of his financial stewardship of his own affairs, but because of his financial stewardship of our affairs, we were living in Dickensian poverty.

The UK's global influence score was harmed by being outside the EU, meaning that its status on international trade had dropped from joint second to 28th, on a par with the bloke down the pub who can get you a telly, no questions asked.

Downing Street sources said they found the findings "strange" and "lacking in evidence", and that they had...alternative facts.

The government responded in time-honoured fashion by blaming disabled benefits cheats. This was undermined by statistics from the government's own Department for Work and Pensions which showed that there were almost no recorded cases of disability fraud in the last financial year.

Disability Living Allowance fraud was just 0.1 percent, which they rounded off to £0m.
Personal Independence Payment cheating was found to be zero percent in the same period.

To crack down on this, the government hired an extra 2,500 people to deal with it.

The nation tried to make sense of that, while trying to make sense of this:
United Utilities declared its intention to pay £339 million of dividends to its shareholders for the last financial year, despite illegally dumping millions of litres of sewage in Lake Windermere, one of the most famous and loved bodies of water in the world.
The increased shareholder payout was substantially more than the £227 million it made in profits.

One of the most polluting water companies in the land was giving its shareholders more in payouts than it made in profits.

A reminder: we are the only country on Earth that has privatised all of its water.

To take our minds off that, Business secretary Kemi Badenoch announced plans to remove red tape for pubs, restaurants and cafes to make the most of "Brexit freedoms" and allow customers to be served outside.
Thanks to us leaving the EU, pavement dining was to become a permanent feature of the high street.

Take that France! In your face Spain!

Europeans could only dream of having the freedom to al fresco.

Fishi Sunak called a general election for July 4th, which would become our Independence From The Tories Day.

He announced the date by marching out of the door of Number 10 and positioned himself at a lectern as what started as a few drops of rain became a deluge that soaked him to the skin, thereby doubling his weight.

He attempted to assure us that the country was safest in his hands, despite being outwitted by the weather.

The spectacle of him getting increasingly dripping wet was accompanied by the strains of the New Labour anthem "Things can only get better", played by ever-present campaigner Steve Bray who briefly became the nation's best DJ.

Furious Conservative MPs, in fear of losing their seats, called him a clown, which is odd. The past 14 years had indicated that they quite enjoyed being led by a clown.

As the election was declared, Britons were urged to stockpile tinned food, batteries and bottled water under a new campaign launched by the UK government to encourage the public to prepare for disasters, like the Tories somehow winning the next election.

The "Prepare" website called on households to stock up on bottled water, non-perishable food, a tin opener, baby supplies and pet food, and if you didn't have a baby or a pet, then you should get yourself at least one of each, which you could eat in an emergency.

On the campaign trail, the Drear Leader Titchy Suitsize was trying to make the impression that he was just your average man of the people by taking a private jet between carefully selected factories to chat with ordinary hard working people who were doing the right thing by working hard.

The PM was quizzed by what seemed to be ordinary workers at West William Distribution in Derbyshire.

Completely at random, Sunak picked one bloke in a hi-viz jacket to ask him the first question, which was "what sets you apart" on improving people's finances?

He might as well have been asked "what makes your hair so shiny and bouncy?"

Another worker thanked Sunak for attending the event as he was a "pretty busy guy right now".

Mr Prime Minster sir...how is it that you are so fabulous and sexy?

Neither of the men mentioned in their questions that they were Conservative councillors, who had been asked to dress up and pretend to be workers, as part of the PM's integrity drive.

Fresh from that success, Sunak went to Barry in south Wales, where he asked people in a brewery if "all the football" of the Euros would be good for revenue.

Which would have gone down better if Wales had qualified for the tournament.

He then stopped off in Belfast, where his people thought that in order to best reflect his buoyant future as leader, he should be photographed at the Titanic Centre.

He then allowed himself to be snapped beneath the sign for The Crooked Billet pub in Worsthorne. The photo released showed him under the sign with "The" and "Billet" out of the frame.

Then on to getting snapped beneath two signs that said "EXIT" and finally to be photographed in front of the supermarket Morrison's logo, his head dividing the sign and obliterating the middle letters to show just the word "moron" either side of his ears.

Other than that, everything was going very well.

The following day, he retreated from the campaign trail to have one of his butlers lick his wounds.

Things got worse for him when it was reported that income growth under the Tories has been the "worst in generations".

The Institute for Fiscal Studies said the average Briton would be almost £5,000 richer if living standards had grown at the rate recorded in the 50 years prior to the Conservatives coming to power in 2010.

And which lefty, woke, Starmer loving paper reported that? The Daily Telegraph!

The average salary in the US was just more than £52,000 last year, according to the US Bureau of

Labor Statistics, while in the UK it was £35,000, according to the Office for National Statistics, and the gap was widening.

During the two decades in which UK wages flatlined, those in the US grew by 20 per cent.

Probably Jeremy Corbyn's fault.

June

Extreme weather continued to ravage parts of Europe, with an excessive heat warning in place in Italy, freak tsunami waves hit the Balearic Islands, there were huge floods in the French Alps and deadly wildfires ripped through Turkish villages.

The mercury rose to 42C in southern Italy, while hotels in Sicily turned tourists away amid a drought on the island.

A freak wave washed away sunbeds in Menorca and torrents of water hurtled down a mountainside in France devastating an Alpine village and forcing its inhabitants to evacuate by helicopter.

In Turkey, a huge wildfire swept through several villages.

In Greece, authorities evacuated several villages south of Athens and in the southern Peloponnese region because of wildfires and streets in Zermatt in Switzerland, under the shadow of the Matterhorn, were left impassable after being deluged with water.

In this country, the Met Office issued a weather warning across parts of the UK as torrential rain and storms sweep the country.
They warned that some homes and businesses could be damaged from flooding or lightning strikes and power outages could occur.

Also, there could be pestilent swarms of deadly insects and the tectonic plates might rupture and huge volcanic eruptions could fill the sky with boiling hot ash that would bring a nuclear winter lasting a hundred years and we were all going to die.

But no-one was bothered about that because...

The 80th D-Day commemoration was held in France in the presence of international leaders such as the President of France and the Chancellor of Germany and the President of the United States of America, who had to travel 3000 miles to get there.

Fishi Sunak, who didn't have to travel at all because he was already there, left early for an interview with ITV News to try and convince us that he was someone we could trust and was in tune with British values.

The solemn event was therefore overshadowed by the actions of one man who has never heard the word "no" in his entire perfumed life and couldn't quite believe that the soldiers who landed on D-Day couldn't have reorganised their diary 80 years ago so as not to clash with his electioneering.

In health news, an urgent warning was issued after an E.coli outbreak was linked to a "nationally distributed food item".

An unspecified number of people were being treated in hospital due to the outbreak, caused by an unspecified item of food.

The UK Health Security Agency said testing indicated that most of the 113 cases reported in the UK were "part of a single outbreak" but did not give more details about the "food item" thought to be responsible.

Shopping was briefly turned into a game: a sort of Supermarket Sweep that might kill you.

In other alarming news, patriotic Brits learned that we had become ever more reliant on imported power to keep the lights on.

Other countries were to supply most of the extra capacity needed to protect the UK from spells of cold and windless weather, the biggest supplier was expected to be France.

We were going to be kept warm with French electricity.

"I'd rather freeze to death", said everyone who was planning to vote Reform.

As a way to entice the public to vote Conservative, they announced a plan to launch a clampdown on "anti-driver" measures including urban 20mph zones and low-traffic neighbourhoods, and roll back the Ulez car tax in London if they won the election.

They wanted faster speeds in built up areas and more pollution.

All of the measures they were proposing were promises to fix the things they had been responsible for breaking.

At the Euro 2024 competition, the German authorities requested that English fans resist the urge to go on about The War and not to be "d**ks".

Impossible, said England fans in Düsseldorf, who were filmed chanting "10 German bombers", sung to the tune of 'If You're Happy and You Know It', referring to German casualties in the Second World War.

It had regularly been heard at England matches, bellowed by morons who think patriotism is getting a cross of St. George tattooed on their foreheads.

A German police chief made the mistake of warning that any supporter seen performing a Nazi salute would be arrested.

Cue thousands of beered up morons doing the Heil Hitler. He doesn't know us very well, does he?

A major breakthrough with potentially life-changing consequences was made in the field of Artificial Intelligence.

The Turing Test was introduced by Second World War codebreaker Alan Turing, who predicted that computers would one day acquire abilities rivalling human intelligence.

The test called for someone to engage in a text-based conversation with another person and a computer. If he could not tell which was which, the computer would pass the test.

Researchers claimed that ChatGPT had become the first AI to pass.

At best this meant that we were all about to be fired and replaced by a computer, at worst it would become self-aware and as those films with Arnold Schwarzenegger demonstrated, it would be curtains for the human race.

Not curtains for the world though, as we pour excrement in the water and pollute the air and ruin the ground for money, the world would probably get along just fine without us.

In law 'n' order news, there wasn't much in the way of it in London.

Crime had soared in the capital after more than 100 local police stations were shut down. Experts wondered if the two could be in any way connected.

The Conservatives, who had been in power for 14 years, were furious and demanded to know who was responsible.

Of the 160 police stations that the city had in 2008, only 36 remained.

Researchers warned that criminals were specifically targeting areas the Met had abandoned.

Among those stations closed, one had been taken over by drug dealers to be used as a weed factory.

As the election drew near, Nigel Farage's Reform was engulfed in a racism storm.

Comments made by canvassers in Clacton, where Farage was running to be an MP, were revealed by an undercover Channel 4 News investigation.

One volunteer was filmed calling the Prime Minister a 'f****** P***' after advocating shooting those arriving by small boat.

People were absolutely stunned to hear that kind of language from a Reform party candidate.

No one could believe their ears when they heard a Reform Party candidate speaking in that way.

The Mail warned its readers not to vote Labour because it could leave taxpayers with a £35m bill for departing Tory MPs.

The Independent Parliamentary Standards Authority estimated that each politician leaving the Commons costs £116,000 on average as we are forced to smooth their passage out of Westminster and into the real world.

Very expensive while they've got the job. Not exactly cheap when they lose it

Meanwhile, the owner of a seaside donkey ride business said he had been forced to weigh children before letting them on the animals due to rising obesity among young kids.

John Nuttall, whose firm operated in Lincolnshire, said youngsters were required to step on a set of scales to ensure they did not break a six-stone (38kg) weight limit.

The 61-year-old said he feared heavier weight loads might harm his mules.

A sign read that riders must be under the age of ten, shorter than 4ft 6in (1.4m) and meet the weight limit before they coud take a £4 trip on the animals.

You shouldn't destroy the health of a donkey if some ass of a parent couldn't control the eating habits of their offspring.

Just a coincidence: analysis showed that companies linked to Conservative donors had collectively received £8.4bn in public money since 2016, more than 150 times what the party had received in support.

It's the best investment you can make.

What else would have made back 150 times what was invested in just eight years?

You'd have to have shares in Taylor Swift to have made out like that.

July

Parts of the country had seen a month's rainfall in the first week of July and flood warnings were sounding.

Southern Europe continued to roast in ferocious heat, with scorching and dry conditions fanning wildfires around the Balkans.

Greece was experiencing record heatwave with temperatures reaching 43C and fires raged in the Peloponnese.

Meanwhile, France saw temperatures rise above 40C in the south.

Tourist hotspots throughout the Med baked, with excessive heat alerts.

In Croatia, the highest-ever temperature in the Adriatic Sea was recorded and a severe drought in Sicily had caused the island's only natural lake to dry up with the Italian government declaring a state of emergency.

But no-one cared about that because...

The election was held and Labour won.

Tories out:

Liz "the Blunder" Truss, Grant "Four Names" Schapps, Penny "Fight" Mordaunt, Johnny Mercer, Alex Chalk, Gillian Keegan, Jacob Ree-Smugg, Lucy Fraser, Michelle Donelan, Mark Harper, Therese Coffey, Robert Buckland, Simon Hart, Simon Clarke, Damian Green.

Survived:

Fishi Sunak, Priti Patel, Jeremy Hunt, Ian Duncan Smith, Cruella Braverman, Claire Coutinho, Tom Tugenhat, James Cleverly, Mel Stride, Oliver Dowden, Victoria Atkins, Esther McVey, Steve Barclay, Laura Trott, Kemi Bad-Enoch, Robert "Murals" Jenrick, Kit Malthouse, Gavin "Shut Up" Williamson and Geoffrey BVI Cox.

Stood down:

Michael "I Love Dancing" Gove.

Several minutes after the result was announced, the nation was appalled at the lack of progress that had been achieved under the new Labour government.

Kier Starmer had been in power for hundreds of seconds and what had he achieved in all that time?

NHS waiting lists were at all time high, schools were falling down, there was sewage in our rivers, children going to bed hungry, wealth inequality was dragging down the country, and Labour had done nothing.

Under his watch, the cost of a pint had never been higher, the bus you were waiting for didn't show up and the summer had been called off due to the rain.

What this country needed was to get our hope back.

The right-wing press spoke for the nation when they said it was time for change. We'd had enough of this failing Labour government, time for a general election.

Jacob Smugg was filmed losing his North East Somerset and Hanham seat, while standing next to Phin 'Barmy Brunch' Adams of the Monster Raving Loony Party at the University of Bath campus. The good people of North East Somerset and Hanham finally woke up from their reverie, came to their senses and kicked out that cartoon posho from the Beano. It only took them 14 years.

Memorably, Phin was wearing a full-face hood, with a baked bean print, with fried eggs for the eyes and a sausage nose. It looked like someone had set his face on fire and put it out with a full English breakfast.

The outgoing Smugg was 55 years old.

Amazing that someone who had only lived that long could be that affected – you'd have thought it would take much longer than that.

During his concession speech, Smugg quoted the 1968 children's classic, Chitty Chitty Bang Bang.

"From the ashes of disaster grow the roses of success", he said.

If you resembled the Child Catcher - all top hat and evil intent, mean and malevolent - you would be best advised to keep well away from anything to do with Chitty Chitty Bang Bang.

Nigel Farage won a seat in parliament on the eighth time of trying. He had shown up in person on the campaign trail and managed to persuade the people of Clacton that he and his millionaire colleagues had their best interests at heart. It was to be one of the last times they would ever see him. He would be henceforth in America, trying to attract Donald Trump's attention and talking for money, while "representing Clacton on the world stage".

Clactonites had done their research and elected the man who, when in the European Parliament, had the worst voting record of any MEP, while he was taking his full salary plus expenses.

Of 746 MEPs, he had the 745th worst record of voting, with only Irish MEP Brian Conley voting fewer times, a man who was paralysed from the waist down.

Not only did Farage fail to vote, his party had the worst attendance record across the whole continent.

Sounds like the perfect candidate to represent our interests, thought the people of Clacton.

Tetchy Sunak was shown the door. Fortunately for him, he had plenty of other doors.

In this country alone, there was his constituency home, a Grade II-listed Georgian Manor house, with a swimming pool, hot tub, yoga studio, gym and tennis court in 12 acres of grounds.

There was also a £7m London mews house and a flat on the Old Brompton Road.

His most valuable asset, though, was his wife's shareholding in Infosys, the Bangalore-based IT company co-founded by her father – riches that neither she nor her husband did anything to acquire. They were just given it.

Their joint wealth was estimated at £651million, and glimpses of their affluence had often been spotted during their time in No10.

Tetchy had previously made headlines with a £3,500 bespoke suit, a £450 pair of Prada loafers, a

£750 backpack, and a £180 'smart' coffee mug.

If he'd let the coffee mug run the country, then he might not have been calling the movers.

Amazing that a three and a half grand suit can be made to look like it was made to measure someone else.

As for his legacy, his time in office saw an unimaginably large mountain of our money just disappear.

Huge amounts went into the pockets of friends of the regime, while he claimed that the public weren't interested in that.

His wife held shares in a company that, through great coincidence, benefitted from government contracts, while he personally caused the Covid death rate to surge by his Eat Out to Help (the Virus) Out.

His inner circle was accused of using inside information to make money on betting on the date of the election and he went to parties while handing out fines to others for sitting on a park bench together, and as the keeper of the nations finances as the Chancellor of the Exchequer, his own wife was registered as living somewhere else for tax purposes.

Integrity, professionalism, accountability.

And this richest of political couples donated a six figure sum to an already rich private school he went to while denying funding to prop up collapsing state schools, and when asked what he would do for young people, cheerfully said: national service.

He announced he would relinquish the leadership of the Conservatives and the Tories engaged in yet another contest for a successor. Who would the geniuses that gave us Liz Truss as PM foist on us next?

The Green Party came second in 40 seats, polling higher than they ever had, almost doubling their previous high tally and then disappeared from view as the nation's media fought to stick a microphone in Nigel Farage's face, or if he was unavailable, then any opaquely funded, right-wing think-tank wonk would do.

The Royal family was delighted to reveal that The Queen and Duke of Edinburgh had become members of Scotland's greatest order of chivalry, The Most Ancient and Most Noble Order of the Thistle.

It wasn't THE Queen, as she had died. This was the other Queen, often referred to as the "not my Queen" Queen.

The Duke of Edinburgh was similarly not THAT Duke, but the artist previously known as Prince Edward.

Remember him?

It is the King who decides who receives the award, and how lucky they were to win this honour, having worked tirelessly to become the King's wife and his brother.

At the ceremony, the royal group was pictured in all their Thistle-related finery; the most ridiculous costumes you'd see outside of a pantomime.

There were velvet cloaks and medals as big as dinner plates and sashes and gold chains so large you could anchor a ship with them, and braids like curtain pulls and floppy Napoleon hats with half a dead ostrich on the top.

They were tottering around in clobber worth the price of semi detached in Ealing, with the self satisfied smiles of people who don't think they look out of place at all in a country where millions of their subjects' children were going to bed hungry and ex-military veterans were sleeping on the streets.

And then they had a procession, because of course they did. They have processions like we take walks.

If they did take a walk somewhere and they weren't accompanied by a marching band they'd wonder if they had gone deaf.

The new PM warned of "tough decisions" ahead. It was to become his mantra, just as "I have been very clear that..." had been the Tories'.

Away from politics, the men's England football team made it an overseas final for the first time.

England secured a showdown against Spain thanks to the referee having been momentarily struck blind and VAR simultaneously breaking down so they missed an obvious handball by Saka and then called the worst penalty decision of all time

I'm sorry, that should have read: England secured a showdown against Spain thanks to Ollie Watkins' stunning last-minute strike against the Netherlands, sealing a 2-1 win.

There, just patriotically fixed that.

Naturally, disappointment was to follow.

There was trouble in paradise, as the majority stockholder of the Reform organisation Nigel Farage effectively sacked his deputy, down to earth man of the people, millionaire property developer Ben Habib.

Down to earth man of the people millionaire ex-City trader Nigel Farage announced a new leadership team, making down to earth man of the people millionaire property developer Richard Tice his deputy.

Down to earth man of the people millionaire ex-Goldman Sachs banker and founder of a concierge service to the super rich, Zia Yusuf was made chairman of the outfit.

Lee Anderthall became Chief Whip.

He was the poorest one of the lot and he made £100,000 a year from his *other* job.

This made the group that portrayed itself as the anti-elite party, the one with the average richest members in parliament.

In a gaffe at the NATO summit, President Joe Biden introduced Ukrainian President Volodymyr Zelensky as "President Putin".

The 81-year-old was facing mounting calls to drop out of the Presidential race because he was old, had a tendency to forget things and lose his train of thought.

Donald Trump, on the other hand was not facing mounting calls to drop out of the race, because he is a Republican and Republicans care about nothing except winning.

Joe Biden had the occasional flub, which was unforgivable to right-wingers.

Donald Trump, on the other hand, had been found liable for sexual abuse and defamation and was ordered to pay more than $80 million in damages to the victim.

Trump had also been found liable for fraud regarding overvaluation of The Trump Organization and his net worth, and was appealing a $364 million fine plus $100 million interest.

He was also convicted on numerous counts of falsifying business records.

He was also facing trial on federal charges related to the attempted coup after losing the 2020 election. He was also expected to go to trial for federal charges relating to his handling of classified documents.

Donald Trump and his businesses had been involved in over 4,000 legal cases, which is not normal.

He ran a Trump University that was found to have defrauded students, and had to pay $25m in restitution.

And there were the numerous accusations of sexual abuse, assault and harassment, some of which he seemed to have boasted about while engaging in "locker room talk".

But it was Joe Biden that Republicans deemed was unfit for office.

As part of our Brexit freedoms, the government authorised use of a pesticide that had been banned in the EU because it killed bees.

The neonicotinoid pesticide Cruiser SB was used on sugar beet and is highly toxic to bees and had the potential to kill off whole populations of the insect.

No problem, said His Majesty's Government, we can do without bees.

Doing without bees would mean that we would be denied the crops that bees pollinate, which would be perfectly fine if you don't like Kiwifruit.

Or potatoes, onions, cashews, celery, strawberries, star-fruit, Brazil nuts, beets, mustard, rapeseed, broccoli, cauliflower, cabbage, brussels sprouts, chinese cabbage, turnips, peas, beans, chilli pepper, red pepper, bell pepper, green pepper, papaya, safflower, caraway, chestnuts, watermelons, tangerines, oranges, grapefruit, coconuts, coffee, coriander, carrots, sunflower, flax, lychee, fennel, macadamias, apples, mangos, passion fruit, avocados, apricots, cherries, almonds, peaches, nectarines, guava, pomegranates, pears, black currants, red currants, tomatoes, grapes, blackberries, elderberries, sesame and cotton.

Now we had our sovereignty back, we'd be fine as long as we didn't want to eat or wear anything.

Margaret Thatcher's experiment to see whether gifting foreign companies a series of monopolies to sell life's most precious substance to a captive consumer who would go to jail for non-payment continued to deliver for those who were lucky enough to be running the businesses.

Thames Water's CEO was handed a huge bonus despite his firm pumping raw sewage into the sea and rivers and racking up a massive debt.

In 2023 there were 16,990 sewage discharges, double the number of the previous year's dismal performance.

Chris Weston, boss of the UK's largest water firm for a mere three months, received a £195,000 bonus despite the company warning it could run out of money with a debt mountain totalling over £15billion,

Weston defended his bonus, saying: "You need to be able to attract the right talent, the best talent to the company and going hand in glove with that is an appropriate remuneration package."

Can these people hear themselves?

The North Paddington food bank (NPFB) in West London launched a campaign urging policymakers to use the millions spent on subsidised catering for parliamentarians to tackle food insecurity.

They wanted MPs to give up a small amount of their vast remuneration and benefits in order to help those less well off.

Funny, no?

As part of the campaign, a fake menu based on the one served to MPs was uploaded to Deliveroo under a listing called "The Houses of Parliament".

Thomas Delap, who runs The North Paddington food bank, said it was galling to think that politicians were "eating like kings" while people were "starving".

The only item actually available to order via Deliveroo was a T-shirt emblazoned with the slogan "common as muck" on the front and "support your local food bank" on the back.

As a science experiment, I noted the food available in Westminster and compared it to the menu in a hotel called the Corinthia. I chose it because it was nearby, it was not as super-fancy as, say, The Ritz and it had a restaurant run by that bloke Tom Kerridge off the telly, and the descriptions of what was on offer were similar, even if the prices were not.

Start with a Martini -

Kerridge's, £17; House of Commons Pugin Room, £6.40.

From the a la carte:

To start:

Members Restaurant of the House of Commons: pan seared scallops with celeriac, green apple, toasted hazelnuts and jus burnt butter...£4.95

Kerridge's: brown crab royale, confit egg yolk, sourdough cracker £24.50

To follow:

House of Commons venison, pan seared red deer with port and juniper braised haunch tartlet, smoked butter mash, black garlic and bordelaise sauce, £14.80

Kerrdige's venison bun, veal sweetbreads, red wine sauce salsa verde, £57.50

For pudding:

House of Commons rich dark chocolate marquise mousse, lightly spiced with cinnamon and orange, warm poached pears and a crème fraiche ice cream, £3.00

Kerrdige's chocolate marquis- kirsch cherries, crème fraiche ice cream, £19.50

To drink:

A nice Australian Shiraz from Barroso valley...House of Commons £27.15.

Kerrdige's, £190.

Eating like an MP was like going back in time to the 1970s.

In the House of Commons you could get a sirloin steak with roast king oyster mushrooms, green beans, French fries, roasted garlic and parsley butter for £13.90

If you went to a Harvesters it would be double that.

MPs also get to put the cab to take them there and back on expenses, and they get the rent and electric and gas paid on the flat they're living in, and they get child support of over 5 grand a year on each of their children, capped at 3 kids, not 2 like for the rest of us, and they're on £91,346 a year plus a quarter of a million pounds in expenses, and they're eating five star food at MacDonald's prices, while complaining that they have to take other jobs outside of their duties as an MP in order to make ends meet.

Are you getting the feeling you've been had yet?

In America, someone took a shot at Donald Trump and missed. His fans declared that God had saved him by turning his head at the precise moment a bullet whizzed by. They did not address why God had not turned his head sufficiently to dodge the bullet entirely. He moves in mysterious ways.

Trump slammed the FBI, as the agency confirmed it was probing whether he was actually hit by a bullet at all.

The theory was that the tiny trickle of red on his face was not blood, but was from ketchup on a chicken wing he had put behind his ear to eat later.

The former peach powder puff President and full time whining baby, Agolf Twitler, staged a dramatic entrance to his Make America White Again rally, waddling into a packed hall of numbskull ding-a-lings to James Brown's "It's a Man's World.".

This was an excellent choice of music because if there's one thing that his Loony Tunes, camo-clad, gun toting, bible bashing cultists in America can agree on, it was that real men put lifts in their shoes and make up on their faces and waft around in a cloud of hairspray while dad-dancing to YMCA.

I can't be sure, but I bet that James Brown would not appreciate his music being used by Mr "good people on both sides".

Trump entered wearing a bandage on his ear, as did the most particularly slack-jawed members of his willingly gullible audience.

They sat there as though in rapture, with huge plasters on the side of their heads, like the idiot crowds in Life of Brian who took off their shoe because Brian lost his while trying to get away from them.

Hulk Hogan, the actor from the pretend wrestling shows, ripped his shirt off on-stage at the rally, in a sort of religious fervour, to reveal a Trump T-shirt underneath and the crowd had a patriotgasm you could hear from space.

It looked like a scene lifted directly from Idiocracy, a film about the lowering of intelligence over time and how America became not a democracy but an idiocracy.

It used to be a comedy about the future, now it was a documentary about the present.

An IT outage sparked chaos as Gay hookup app Grindr crashed after a spike of users around Milwaukee, the location of the Republican National Convention (RNC).

Ex-Congressman George Santos posted a video on social media claiming "Grindr executives are calling the RNC convention the Grindr Superbowl".

Gay hookup sites had spiked around gatherings of Republicans in the past.

Users reported an increase in traffic around the Conservative Political Action Conference outside Washington, D.C. in March last year and Grindr had shared data with news sites on the app's use around the 2016 RNC in Cleveland, Ohio.

On the night check-in for the convention began, Grindr found a 120 percent increase in online users in the area.

The New York Post reported rent boys were also doing a brisk trade.

"Business has been way better. I've seen 10 clients so far," one male escort told the paper.

He said they were mostly married white men between the ages of 40 and 50.

However, female escorts said they were making less money than usual.

The Republicans' credo: don't do who we do, do as we say.

In Britain, five Just Stop Oil activists received record sentences for planning to block M25.

Five years in prison for attending a meeting aimed at drawing the government's attention to the climate catastrophe we appeared to be walking towards

Meanwhile water companies had doled out £85 billion in dividends, loaded the industry with £64 billion in debt, dumped sewage for 4.6m hours in 2023 alone and what happened? Nothing.

Meanwhile, King Charles was doing his bit.

Two state Bentleys were to undergo a green makeover by being converted to run on biofuel as part of the monarch's eco-drive.

But the King wasn't stopping there. He was also going to upgrade his 2 helicopters so they run on less fuel.

That's right – in order to have a lower carbon footprint, his majesty was getting 2 new helicopters, bought by us, on the presumption that they're more eco-friendly.

The man lives in 3 palaces, 3 castles the size of palaces, and enough lodges, cottages, parks, halls and houses to sleep an army.

All of which are staffed, cleaned, heated and secured all year, every year, to His Majesty's precise specifications.

But he once turned off a light when he was leaving a throne room, so he's saving the planet.

The Olympics opened in Paris and the world's greatest athletes gathered to demonstrate the best of humankind.

The worst of humankind, eager to be outraged, took such offence at the opening ceremony that they almost turned themselves inside-out they were so furious.

August

UK households were urged not to kill flies or any other insect because studies revealed an 80% decline in bug life over the past twenty years.

While they might be annoying, and ruin the odd barbecue, we would miss them when they're gone.

Meanwhile, Jaguar Land Rover was among a string of luxury carmakers to be hit by major disruption after flooding in Switzerland paralysed a top aluminium producer.

Following heavy rainfall and flooding in parts of central Europe, Novelis, a manufacturer that runs a mill in the alpine city of Sierre, was forced to shut down operations at the end of June. Porsche, BMW and Mercedes were also affected.

Adele's concert plans were called into question after the singer was forced to cancel the final dress rehearsal for her Munich concert after reports of fierce thunderstorms and heavy rain.

The previous week was the Earth's hottest day on record, according to both the EU's Copernicus Climate Change Service and the US's NASA.

For those that don't believe in science, there was the unavoidable effects of climate change in the soaring price of insurance coverage.

Home insurers, hit by a rash of extreme weather events, last year suffered their worst net underwriting loss this century.

In America alone, it was the fourth consecutive year in which insurance losses from natural disasters topped $100bn.

That will show up on your next insurance premium.

Global warming does not mind whether you believe in it or not. It's going to affect you anyway.

No-one cared about that, however, because…

Violence broke out in Southport after misinformation spread online about the killing of three young girls.

Stoked by a certain frog-faced gasbag, the riots saw police officers hospitalised after being attacked by bricks and other missiles, property was destroyed, cars set alight and local people were terrified by gangs of easily led, mouth-breathing morons, who were patriots showing how much they love their country.

None of the fomenters of the violence were sanctioned or punished in any way.

In other crime news, Just Stop Oil protesters were jailed for up to five years for a blockade which interrupted the flow of traffic on the M25.

That absolutely anything at all, including a light breeze, seems to interrupt the flow of traffic on the M25 did not matter to the judge who told the defendants as he handed down the sentences that their behaviour was "disproportionate to your aims".

New research revealed what grown-ups have always known instinctively, that the kids are a huge disappointment.

Children used to want to grow up to be an astronaut. Now they want to be an influencer.

They want to do a little dance on TikTok and make a million pounds.

As a back-up plan, the next most popular profession was inhabiting a character costume in a theme park.

I am not making that up.

In theory, it is a terrific wheeze, what with the free entry and queue-jumping staff tickets for the rides on your days off.

In practice, they might change their minds when they climb into a heavy nylon bear suit in the baking hot summer sun. Imagine the smell, apart from anything else.

Speaking of aromas, Chancellor Rachel Reeves attempts to add a feminine touch to her private Treasury bathroom were scuppered by a large bill to cover up a urinal.

The facility had been used by Winston Churchill, who was presumably so busy that he not have time to raise a toilet seat.

The press had a fit you could hear through a tiled wall.
How dare a mere woman, a Labour woman at that, contemplate the removal or covering up of a porcelain pee receptacle that had been on the receiving end of our greatest Britain?

Reeves, who was Britain's first female chancellor since the office was set up more than 800 years previously, was told she could not remove the 100-year-old urinal from her private bathroom and was been quoted at least £8,000 to seek permission to build a permanent cover over it.

That was £8000 for seeking permission. To actually cover it up was extra.

It sounded like the people she asked just thought of a number, doubled it and added a zero on the end. It is probably why it costs £11,000 pounds to change a lightbulb on an aircraft carrier.

Putting the potty row behind her, the Chancellor set off on a three-day tour of North America to sell the UK as a "safe haven" for international investors and financiers.

While she was telling Wall Street bosses, Canadian pension funds and clean energy companies how well ordered a place this country was, the news was full of exciting videos of rioting in cities throughout the land.

While trying to sell Britain as a secure bet for investment, her message was undermined by very British morons with swastika tattoos throwing bricks through Gregg's windows, stealing bath bombs from Lush and upgrading their phones for free by raiding an O2 store, while rolling bins on fire toward police lines and setting a hotel ablaze.

Social media lit up with videos of cretinous oafs getting hit by bricks thrown by their own side, while toothless troglodytes yelled something about wanting their country back.

Reeves dismissed the protests and insisted that the images of police clashes and far-right chants would not tarnish Britain's international reputation, as the Canadian government updated travel advice for its citizens, warning visitors about travelling to the UK.

Back home, the race to be the next leader of the Conservative Party was on and the public was not enthused.

Three in five Brits did not care who becomes the next Tory leader, according to a poll showing a high level of public apathy.

After 14 years of the clown show, we were too exhausted to care.

All we wanted to know was that they were gone and that we weren't being gas lit every single day by a regimented troop of nodding dogs who got sent out to tell us up is down and they are investing more on everything than any government in history, and that nothing bad was ever their fault.

The characters lining up to replace Titchy Suitsize, was a whole cartoon villain list of deplorables and unmentionables and some that most of us wouldn't have been able to pick out of a line up.

They were Kemi Badenoch, James Cleverly, Robert Jenrick, Priti Patel, Mel Stride and Tom Tugendhat.

It looked like auditions for a new Adams Family film.

All we knew was that the final choice was to be made by the membership of the Tory Party, those geniuses who brought us Prime Minister Liz Truss.

What could possibly go wrong?

Talking of the Blundertruss - Liz left the stage in a huff at an event to promote her own book after campaigners unfurled a flag behind her.

The former PM, who lasted 45 disastrous days in office, was in Suffolk when the campaign group Led By Donkeys lowered a remote-controlled banner emblazoned with the phrase: "I crashed the economy" below a picture of a lettuce.

She said the prank was "not funny", which in itself was very funny.

Not content with being embarrassed by others, she embarrassed herself by posting on social media that Led By Donkeys were "far-left activists" who used the stunt as a means to "intimidate people and suppress free speech".

Free-speech was OK with Liz, but only up to a point, which rather missed the essence of it being "free".

The Labour government was getting down to business. They set about solving some of the rolling strikes that the country had been suffering from under the previous management.

This made Tory MPs very angry.

The Labour Government was "throwing money at its union paymasters like confetti", they roared, after it had agreed a pay deal with train drivers. They're not worth it, they said.

The people doing the complaining had spent the past 14 years throwing money at their friends and donors like confetti after agreeing that those people *were* worth it.

Man of the people Nigel Farage released his employment and earnings, as required of a member of parliament.

It listed about 130 hours of work per month outside of his duties as an MP, duties which he took very seriously.

Aside from his very important television work, most eye-catchingly, there was the sum of £32,836 from a private donor for travel to America and accommodation.

The purpose of the visit was "To support a friend who was almost killed and to represent Clacton on the world stage".

Sad that the tangerine hued "friend" could not find time in his busy schedule of braying at crowds and cheating at golf to meet Nigel, who had selflessly travelled so far to be by his side.

In music news, revellers at the Leeds festival were told to stay in their tents as Storm Lilian brought 80mph winds.

Liam Gallagher was the star turn, so they didn't miss much, apart form a tidal wave of bad attitude from a zipped-up cagoule, whining into a microphone that had been set about a foot too high.

Videos showed punters clinging to their tents as some flew sky-high.

The tents, not the punters.

One festival-goer described it as "the worst day ever". Literally no-one in the history of humankind had ever suffered so much.

In a "Brexit's going great" development, a poll found that 58% of Brits thought a youth mobility scheme with the EU would be a good idea. Just 10% did not like the sound of it.

The 10% shouted the loudest, and these days, whoever has the loudest voice wins.

The majority wanted to give young people back the freedoms they once had.

Starmer refused because Sid and Ethel in Clacton wouldn't like it because they fear that immigrants might come round their way...an area that is 97% white British.

The Clacton representative was sharing the good news about his constituency with Scottsdale, Arizona.

As part of his duties as an MP for one of England's most deprived areas, he was in America again, for the second occasion in the month, this time addressing a "Keep Arizona Free" summit.

His time was not free. He was paid around £12,000 for a speech.

What he could tell Arizona about Arizona was apparently worth that much.

He defended his decision to go, saying it was booked "over a year ago" and that "I am not the sort of person who lets people down otherwise you get a terrible reputation"!

One of Fauxrage's close political allies revealed that Trump had promised to visit the Reform leader in Clacton.

Andy Wigmore said he attended a meeting in which the Republican nominee vowed to come to the UK and take in the sights of the run-down coastal town.

If only there was some indication as to whether Trump was a truthful person, Clacton could start buying the bunting in anticipation.

Trump's last visit was in 2019, when he dressed as a podgy penguin theme park character for a state dinner and, when inspecting the troops, performed a total eclipse of the Queen by waddling ahead of her and obscuring her from the cameras.

A book by Craig Brown suggested that the Queen confided to a lunch guest that she found him very rude and also believed that Trump must have some sort of arrangement with his wife Melania, or else why would she have remained married to him?

Trump declared that, on the contrary, the Queen had in fact thought most highly of him and that she enjoyed his company more than any president she had ever met, "believe me".

Also, his wife loved him very much. Her affection was so great and all-encompassing that she could hardly bear living in the same state as him.

At a popular Cornwall restaurant a couple were accused of being involved in the worst executed crime ever.

The scene of the incompetence was the Mackerel Sky Seafood Bar and Shack, a name that must have been a task for the sign writer to fit on the one awning.

After running up a bill of £62, a couple were shown on the restaurant's CCTV system leaving their table without paying for their meal.

Not only had they chosen to dine-and-dash on camera, owner Jamie said the couple had left behind their phone number having rang the restaurant earlier to ask whether there were any spare tables.

The restaurant does not even take reservations, it's first come first served and these numpties called to book, left their number and when they got there sat under a CCTV camera in very loud easily recognisable clothes.

The female suspect was wearing a pink hooded top, blue jeans and white shoes and a large white handbag, with which she could have blended in at a Katie Price house-warming do, but not in a fish restaurant in Cornwall.

After they left without paying, owner Jamie posted CCTV images of the couple on his restaurant's Facebook page after which the couple laid low.

I'm kidding, of course they didn't.

The couple complained about their images being loaded onto the internet and allegedly told him they did not enjoy his food, despite the footage showing they cleaned their plates.

Devon and Cornwall Constabulary said: "Police are aware of an incident where two individuals left the Mackerel Sky Seafood Bar and Shack in Newlyn without paying their bill. Enquiries into this matter are ongoing."

Also, anyone with any information that may assist the owner shortening the name of his restaurant should let the authorities know by the usual means.

In Wales, a cycling race was shortened and re-routed because the support vehicles could not keep up with the cyclists due to the country's new default 20mph speed limit.

Wales' Transport Secretary Ken Skates admitted that the policy was so unpopular even his own family had signed the petition against it.

An unpopular policy that makes towns nicer to live in for pedestrians, which every car driver becomes the moment they get out of their vehicles. That makes sense.

The race started in Brynmawr and finished in Monmouthshire.

Englander's wondered whether Monmouthshire couldn't lend Brynmawr some vowels.

Energy bills were announced to be going up by the regulator Ofgem which said that rising prices in the international energy market was the chief driver of this increase.

In other news, energy companies had made £30.5 billion profit since the energy crisis started. Energy distribution companies had increased their profits by 800% in three years.

The companies that make electricity and drill the oil and gas had made £420.4 billion in profits since April 2020.

Apparently that was not enough, so we poor dopes who pay taxes had to stump up more.

Our attention was taken from all that by Robert F Kennedy Jr, who was standing for President of the USA as an independent.

He had made a name for himself as an anti-vaxxer during the pandemic. At one event he compared the US government's use of vaccine mandates to laws in Nazi Germany.

"Even in Hitler's Germany, you could cross the Alps into Switzerland, you could hide in an attic like Anne Frank did", he said.

Kennedy disclosed that a parasitic worm once entered his brain and died, a period that led to "brain fog" and "having trouble with word retrieval and short-term memory," he said.
Later in the campaign, he sidestepped accusations published in Vanity Fair that he sexually assaulted a former nanny, telling a podcast he had "many skeletons in my closet", and that, "I'm no a church boy".
He was later to be introduced as the new president's health czar.
This was NFA – normal for America.

Kier Starmer had walked into a lot of trouble. It was found that he had accepted gifts of some clothes, glasses and tickets to a concert by this year's Most Fabulous Person: Taylor Swift.

He was the most corrupt Prime Minister in the history of this country, declared Conservative MPs, at least it sounded like that was what they were saying, it was hard to hear them behind the mountain of money they had siphoned off from their time in office.

On the American campaign trail, Donald Trump was being presidential.

He wondered aloud whether his opponent Kamala Harris was really black, said she had the laugh of a lunatic and declared that he was "a better looking person".

While giving an interview at the National Association of Black Journalists, he said that he did not know that she was black until a couple of years previously, when "she happened to turn black, and now she wants to be known as black",

At a rally in Pennsylvania, Trump went as far as rambling about rambling.

"I don't ramble. I'm a really smart guy, you know, really smart. I don't ramble. But the other day, anytime I hit too hard, they say he was rambling, rambling," he told the crowd.

Trump said every presidential candidate should be required to take a cognitive test. Pressed this week by CBS News on whether he has done so himself, Trump claimed to have recently had a "perfect score" on two cognitive tests.

"I got everything right. And one of the doctors said, 'I've never seen that before, where you get everything right,'" he said.

This was as believable as anything else he had ever said.

As though Britain was falling behind in the field of embarrassing political news, Esther McVey, the ex-Minister for Common Sense tweeted in answer to a graduated smoking ban:

"First they came for the Communists

And I did not speak out

Because I was not a communist

Then they came for the Jews

And I did not speak out

Because I was not a Jew

Then they came for me

And there was no one left To speak out for me

Pertinent words re Starmer's smoking ban"

These were the words of Martin Niemöller's 1946 poem First They Came, about inaction from within Germany against the Nazis.

She was roundly condemned and withdrew the tweet and apologised.

Just kidding, she said "Nobody is suggesting that banning smoking outside pubs can be equated with what happened to the Jews at the hands of the Nazis. It is ridiculous for anyone to even suggest that was what I was doing", despite it looking as though that is what she was doing.

This was NFE: normal for Esther.

Starmer's plan was to ban smoking in beer gardens, among other crowded outdoor spaces.

Right-wing MPs went berserk, almost as though they were being paid by tobacco companies.

The press went in search of furious smokers and found one in the form of Glynis, a 68 year old who said from within a cloud of poison, "you'll be paying for fresh air next".

It did not look as though she had ever experienced fresh air.

Glynis said she was determined to continue smoking, no matter what.

Glynis had the smoking related severe lung condition Chronic Obstructive Pulmonary Disease.

I am not making that up.

In "why does he hate our country?" news, Kier Starmer had the huge portrait of Margaret Thatcher moved from his study, where her glowering had made it hard for him to think.

That story in a nutshell: man decided to change the decoration in his home without needing to employ an interior designer and without spending £250,000 on gold wallpaper, without knowing who was going to pay for it, but banking on it not being him.

"Traitor!", yelled the press.

Starmer's deputy, Angela Rayner was castigated for having the temerity to enjoy herself while there was suffering in the world.

The deputy PM and housing secretary was filmed dancing with the Australian DJ Fisher in front of a vast crowd at the Hi Ibiza superclub.

Former Tory MP Nadine Dorries penned an article saying that Ms Rayner's behaviour "demeans her office".

This was the same Nadine Dorries who had absented herself from parliament to appear on TV show I'm a Celebrity Get Me Out Of Here, during which she ate a camel's toe and an ostrich's anus.

Rayner found an unlikely defender in Michael Gove, who said, "Angela Rayner is absolutely not my political cup of tea (or even my political glass of Sangria) but all right-wingers criticising her for dancing in Ibiza need to lighten up."

"I'm always glad when politicians take some time off and rest. Plus… she's a pretty good dancer", said Michael Gove, no stranger to the dance himself.

He had memorably been filmed waving his arms in the air like he just didn't care at a Scottish tecno club.

Some said that he had tried to avoid paying the £5 entry fee by stating that he was the Chancellor of the Duchy of Lancaster, which, having seen the video of him prancing around the dance-floor, wasn't the funniest thing about it.

September

The Brazilian rainforest was starved of rain and stretches of the Amazon River had dried up in the midst of a protracted drought.

Bone dry vegetation created tinder-like conditions.

It was a similar story in the Pantanal region, the world's largest tropical wetland, and in one week week, more than 60% of Brazil was enveloped in smoke.

Meanwhile, floods killed at least 384 people in Myanmar, 21 in central Europe, 10 in Morocco and six in Japan.

Storm Boris ravaged countries including, but not limited to, Poland, the Czech Republic, Romania, Austria and Italy, leading to billions of pounds of damage, which certainly sounds like Boris.

In Britain, it was announced that the summer just gone had been the hottest in recorded history and we'd had the hottest day ever.

Also, we had suffered the wettest August ever with some places getting double the entire summer rainfall in that one month.

This is exactly as scientists had predicted would happen with global warming, but no-one was interested in that because...

The prison population had reached a new high and ministers did not rule out sending overflow lags to Estonia.

This is perfectly normal in a well-run country.

The Tories, who had been in uninterrupted power for 14 years, blamed Labour for not having fixed everything that was wrong in the land on day one of Kier Starmer's premiership.

In Russia, an MP called Lt-Gen Andrei Gurulev told us that Vladimir Putin would give Brits "three days to leave UK" before hitting the island with an atomic tsunami, which was very nice of him.

Good to be forewarned.

He went on to taunt us Brits, laughing: "Swim, swim, swim".

In these brown waters? He must be joking.

Proud Brits need fear no enemy, however, as we were a sea faring nation that ruled the waves.

We had ships and submarines in impressive numbers, or at least they were impressive until you realised none of them actually worked.

Not one of our six attack submarines were at sea.

Only nine out of 25 warships and attack – as opposed to nuclear – submarines are active or deployed.

The rest of the fleet had racked up 30 years of missed days at sea as vessels were either broken down, being modified or undergoing trials.

Assault ship HMS Bulwark and destroyer HMS Daring had both been inactive for more than seven years.

The submarine HMS Ambush has apparently been idle for 765 days

That's just embarrassing. The names, I mean.

Bulwark, Daring and Ambush.

Inactive, Idle and Mothballed, more like.

The most hyped music event of the year was the Oasis get-together, after the warring Gallagher brothers had put their differences aside in the interests of making a lot of money.

Their fans were unamused to see how much the tickets cost and complained loudly on social media. Liam, on brand, tweeted that one disgruntled fan should "shut up" and told another to buy "kneeling tickets".

Ticketmaster had been criticised for applying "dynamic pricing" to the event. This is usually used by cab companies to send the price of a trip skywards when there's a lot of demand, but as the demand for tickets was enormous from the start and sold out immediately, it was difficult to see how dynamic pricing was appropriate here.

It was like saying that the price of pudding in a restaurant should go up if everybody wants it after the main course.

Buyers came to regret that they had been propelled by the confected frenzy to spend way over the odds. Then the radio started playing Oasis hits on a loop and they remembered what a whiny drone they make and then they recalled how boring a live act they are and resentment became the emotion of the day.

In the race to be the next leader of the Conservative Party, Robert Jenrick's fundraising was eclipsing his rivals.

Jenrick raised £250,000 by the end of August, while his nearest competitor, Kemi Badenoch, reached about £200,000.

There was a reason why they needed that much cash just to present themselves to the massed ranks of harrumphing Tory members, the old geezers and their good lady wives who prop up the bar at the golf club.

Under the Conservative Party's rules, those who make it to the final four would have to hand £50,000 to the party. The two candidates who make it to the final round after the party's conference in October would have to sign a further cheque for £150,000 to Conservative campaign headquarters.

That sounded about right.

Start by being beholden to the super-rich donor class early, so as to get used to it in office.

It's the party with corruption actually written into its rule book.

In the other race to be leader, 3000 miles away, at the Economic Club of New York, Donald Trump was asked whether he would commit to making childcare affordable, and what "specific piece of legislation" he would support to do so.

A two-minute, 362-word response followed.

Trump said: "Well, I would do that, and we're sitting down, and I was, somebody, we had Senator

Marco Rubio, and my daughter Ivanka was so impactful on that issue. It's a very important issue. But I think when you talk about the kind of numbers that I'm talking about, that, because, look, child care is child care is. It's, couldn't, you know, there's something, you have to have it. In this country you have to have it."

"But when you talk about those numbers compared to the kind of numbers that I'm talking about by taxing foreign nations at levels that they're not used to — but they'll get used to it very quickly – and it's not gonna stop them from doing business with us, but they'll have a very substantial tax when they send product into our country. Those numbers are so much bigger than any numbers that we're talking about, including child care, that it's going to take care.

"We're gonna have — I, I look forward to having no deficits within a fairly short period of time, coupled with the reductions that I told you about on waste and fraud and all of the other things that are going on in our country, because I have to stay with child care. I want to stay with child care, but those numbers are small relative to the kind of economic numbers that I'm talking about, including growth, but growth also headed up by what the plan is that I just, that I just told you about.

"We're gonna be taking in trillions of dollars, and as much as child care is talked about as being expensive, it's relatively speaking not very expensive compared to the kind of numbers we'll be taking in. We're going to make this into an incredible country that can afford to take care of its people, and then we'll worry about the rest of the world. Let's help other people. But we're going to take care of our country first. This is about America first. It's about Make America Great Again. We have to do it because right now we're a failing nation, so we'll take care of it."

Some people in the audience actually applauded at that point.

Maybe they were just relieved he had stopped speaking.

Back home, the National Trust asked its members to vote on whether to make 50% of the food in its cafes vegetarian as part of its committent to reach net zero by 2030.

This was the worst thing that the Telegraph and the Mail had heard in all the years they had been in print.

They had to build another wing on the internet to accommodate the furious columns they wrote about this, all along the lines of: lefty woke commie socialists are ruining this country.

The food at the National Trust's cafes was already 40% veggie and had been for quite some time, so you would not think an extra 10% would be such a cause for concern. And you would be wrong.

This was an outrage the likes of which the nation had never seen. The purple faced fury brigade had a fit you could see through concrete.

Among those addressing this affront to everything that was decent and patriotic was Jacob Smugg who claimed that it was a silly, attention seeking proposal, and he should know, being an expert in silly attention seeking.

TV farmer Gareth Wyn Jones described the charity's aspiration to provide more plant-based food choices as "absolutely ridiculous from a massive landowner with so many livestock farming families living off these farms".

I'm no expert on TV farmer Gareth Wyn Jones, whose work I was unfamiliar with, nor am I an expert on farming itself, but I think that farms also grow vegetables. I could be wrong.

Nevertheless, it was nice that those who had momentarily tired of shouting at rainbows now had another hobby – shouting at vegan scones.

It's good to diversify.

In America, the Screaming MeMe, Donald Trump, sought to explain that his ramblings were, in fact, nothing of the sort and were a demonstration of his genius.

Trump assured supporters in Pennsylvania that what might look like incoherency, as he frequently departed from his scripted speech, were instead indicators of a brilliance that impressed other great minds.

"I do the weave. You know what the weave is? I'll talk about, like, nine different things that they all come back brilliantly together. And it's like friends of mine that are like English professors, they say: 'It's the most brilliant thing I've ever seen."

He has "friends"?

Even his cult fans weren't buying that one.

In other clown show news, just when we had thought humour had gone out of politics, with Kier "Serious" Starmer, the Conservative Party reminded us what we'd been missing since we had jettisoned them from Number 10.

For membership of the cross party Modernisation Select Committee, the Tories put forward the veteran parliamentary objector Christopher Chope.

Looking for a fresh start, a renewal, to turn a corner and appeal to the youthful, they chose the fustiest, oldest, most determinedly ripe, to the point of going off, old geezer to be a part of parliament's modernisation programme.

They might as well have opened a disco and asked Smugg to be in charge of the music and Therese Coffey to be a go-go girl.

The Tories were reverting to type and being as difficult as possible, like babies who had thrown their rattle out the pram because they were not in charge any more and were going to do everything they could to obstruct the Labour government.
Not for the people's benefit, but for their own childish gratification.
It was selfish, entitled and superior, which was them to a tee.

In Downing Street Kier Starmer decided to buy a Siberian kitten for his family to enjoy.

Sadly, already in residence was Larry the Number 10 cat.

Larry was 17 years old and had seen it all. He had outlasted five Prime Ministers: David Cameron, Theresa May, Boris Johnson, Liz Truss and Rishi Sunak.

At a dinner in Glasgow, Scottish Secretary Ian Murray branded Larry a "little s**t"

"Larry the cat is the most miserable animal you'll ever meet in your life", he said.

Could that in any way be connected to having to live with David Cameron, Theresa May, Boris Johnson, Liz Truss and Rishi Sunak?

In other pet news, presidential candidate Donny the Tangerine Tantrum told his rally crowd in Ohio that Haitians were eating them.

"In Springfield, they are eating the dogs. The people that came in, they are eating the cats. They're eating – they are eating the pets of the people that live there", he said.

Residents in Springfield, the Springfield City Commission, the local police and the Mayor's office all said "oh no they're not" but no one cared about facts.

Facts were old hat.

Nigel Farage was spending more time in the air flying to America than on the ground in Clacton.

He went to the US again, on his third visit there in little more than the two months since he had been elected MP.

He really was representing Clacton on the American stage.

Americans must have be sick of all that talk about Clacton

Farage was listed as the main speaker at a benefit event for the Heartland Institute, an Illinois-based right-wing think-tank which was a denier of human-created climate change.

Tables at the dinner cost up to $50,000 each to reserve.

They didn't say how much it cost to NOT go.

On one of his flying visits to the UK, Farage explained that for "security reasons" he would be doing all constituency meetings over Zoom and not holding any in-person surgeries in Clacton-on-Sea.

He confirmed that the Speaker's Office had advised him to do that.

The Speaker's Office said "oh no we didn't".

Who to believe?

At their conference, the Reform Party were flogging MAGA style hats and "Let's save Britain" T-shirts that were made in Bangladesh.

They were helping make Bangladesh great again.

Farage said the opening of the Birmingham gathering was "the day our party comes of age".

By the looks of the crowd, the age was about 130 years old.

Farage hailed what he said was "the most joyous gathering of a political party I reckon has ever happened in this country in modern history".

This was true, because if there was one thing that Lee Anderson, Anne Widdecombe and Richard Tice conjured in the mind, it was joy.

Shortly after delivering his keynote speech at the National Exhibition Centre, the 60-year-old Farage was back on stage for what organisers called an "evening gala party".

Worst. Party. Ever.

As a band played the Frankie Valli hit "Can't Take My Eyes Off You", Nigel sung along.

If Frankie Valli had been dead, he'd have been spinning in his grave.

Don't tell him about it because it might kill him.

They should have chosen that other Frankie Valli hit: Grease is the Word

As the song reached its chorus, Farage threw his arms around as he danced across the stage.

Once seen, it could not be unseen.

Imagine a man trying to pop imaginary balloons while coping with a stone in his shoe.

At other times, it was more like a series of straight-arm closed-fist salutes while being electrocuted.

You know...joy.

In the art world, there was a lot of soup.

Three Just Stop Oil supporters threw soup over two of Vincent van Gogh's paintings just hours after fellow activists were jailed for doing the same thing to his Sunflowers.

There was a protective glass layer in front of the pictures, and no masterpiece was damaged in the making of this protest.

One soup thrower was jailed for two years.

A two-year prison sentence for throwing condensed soup at a plate of glass.

No punishment whatsoever for a Tory MP dodging £3.7m tax bill, none for selling hundreds of millions of pounds of dud PPE to the NHS, none for dumping billions of litres of sewage in rivers and none for knowingly fitting flammable cladding to tower blocks of flats.

What a way to run a country, eh?

October

England suffered its second worst harvest on record, as in ever.

Heavy rain last winter hit production of wheat and oats.

Those same conditions also hit the rapidly developing UK wine industry, with producers saying harvests were down by 75%.

The price of one of Jacob Rees-Mogg's pints of wine was going to go through the roof.

Meanwhile, the Sahara was under water, tornados and hurricanes were striking Florida, Greece was warning tourists that storms could ruin their holidays by lifting their towels off their sun loungers and everything that climate scientists said would happen eventually, was happening now.

In America, the weather was making some people stupid, or at least, it wasn't making them smarter.

Republican representative and chief ding-a-ling Marjorie Tylor Green said that the hurricane affecting the southern states was created by the Democrats to prevent Republicans from voting. Meteorologists subsequently said that they had received death threats for causing the weather they were reporting on.

I am not making that up.

Hurricane Kirk barrelled across the Atlantic to a sodden Britain that had faced days of flash flooding after torrential rain, but no-one was interested in that because...

The government was introducing a worker's rights bill, which included a small 77p raise in the minimum hourly wage. Bosses of multinational corporations queued up to say how terrible this would be for growth and that they could not afford it.

Tesco, one of the companies that were warning that improved workers' pay would hurt profits also announced that their sales had risen to only £31.5 billion in the six months to August, leaving them with a mere £1.4 billion half year profit.

The person explaining their precarious position was the chief executive who had to struggle by on only a 100% pay rise from the previous year, which took his remuneration to a miserable £10 million.

How does he manage?

In other terrible news for those just about getting by, the commie, socialist, lefty, woke Labour government pressed ahead with plans to charge VAT on private school fees.

One source at a major public school explained that some fee-paying establishments were having to put plans to build new swimming pool complexes and astro-turf pitches on hold because of it.

Children in state schools were being taught in porta-cabins because their asbestos ridden buildings were collapsing, but at least they weren't having new sporting complexes put on hold, because there weren't any plans to build any.

Private schools complained that parents would have to take their children out of their establishments and slum it in state schools, an argument undermined by their insistence that they would take on more pupils to cover the tax bill.

A manager of a good schools guide said that, in order to make ends meet, private school pupils might even have to abandon personalised stationery.

Kemi Badenoch criticised the Labour leader Kier Starmer for using a donor's flat during the general election campaign.

She said that while staying at a wealthy Tory donor's house that she was using during the Conservative leadership campaign.

The donor was one of those climate change deniers that occupy the opaquely funded think-tanks of 55 Tufton Street.

They have names like Net Zero Watch and the Global Warming Policy Foundation. Names that sound like they are concerned for the plight of the little people, and that they know what they're talking about.

Their every utterance disproved both notions.

The GWPF director suggested that it was extraordinary that anyone would believe that there was a climate crisis when carbon dioxide had been mis-labelled as pollution, when it was, in fact, a benefit to the planet.

This is true in much the same way that water is a benefit to humans, until you start drowning in it.

Kier Starmer decided to relinquish control of the Chagos Islands, four years after the United Nation's special international maritime court in Hamburg rejected the notion that it was ours to give away.

In the 1970s, 2,000 Chagos islanders had been rounded up and deported from their own land by Britain so that we could lease it to the Americans to site weapons of mass destruction in Paradise.

Tories harrumphed that we were trading away our sovereignty, forgetting that the Tories themselves had been negotiating returning the islands to its people for years, talks started by James Cleverly, who was competing to be the next Tory leader.

This was the same James Cleverly who was pictured at the Wimbledon finals the previous year. A Tory loophole meant he did not have to declare the freebie as he was there in his capacity as a minister, though quite how watching tennis was vital to his duties as Foreign Secretary remain unclear.

He stated that he was there alone, yet an eager reporter at The Mirror unearthed pictures of him sitting in the posh seats next to his good lady wife.

The official hospitality record released by the Foreign Office states "no" in the section asking whether a spouse, family member or friend joined him.

In the photos Mr Cleverly is shown sitting next to his wife, Mrs Cleverly, who was wearing a fetching pink top and sunglasses above Centre Court.

Or it could have been someone else's wife

Those were the choices…either he was with his wife and said he wasn't, or he was there with someone else's wife, in which case Mrs Cleverly might want a word.

A spokesmodel for the minister claimed that his failure to declare his wife was there was a mistake.

So many mistakes.

James Cleverly later said that he would not stop accepting gifts as the problem was not the accepting, the problem lay with not properly declaring them.

Exactly.

In the race to be chief Tory, Robert Jenrick was in the lead. He had acquired a bovver-boy haircut and had managed to lose enough body fat to make it look suspiciously like he had used the drug of the year, Ozempic, the wight loss regimen for those who don't want to follow a weight loss regimen.

In attempting to attract the eye of party members, he had swung so far to the right that, had he been afloat, he would have circumnavigated the globe.

He declared that if he were elected leader, he would welcome Nigel Farage to the party, leave the European Convention on Human Rights and vote for Donald Trump.

Further, he would ban the colour green, make smiling illegal and re-do Disney's Bambi to include a torture scene before its mother gets shot.

The space on the right of the party was getting quite congested, so as a further inducement to grass-roots conference goers, he revealed that he had given his daughter the middle name of "Thatcher".

That's true commitment. That's going all-in.

The Hammer House of Horrors that was the six candidates was whittled down to just four, amid a total lack of interest in the country at large, which had had enough of the lot of them.

A poll found that more people had heard of Philip Schofield's return to TV in the programme Cast Away, than were aware that there even was a Tory leadership contest.

Liz Truss was conducting a world tour to show just what we were missing not having her as leader. In Australia, she said that in the interests of free speech, state broadcasters should be defunded and that despite the Tories having their bottoms handed to them at the last election, that the public was on their side.

In the American state of Oklahoma, bids opened for a contract to supply the state Department of Education with 55,000 Bibles.

The state Superintendent said he wanted a bible in every classroom, but not any old bible.

According to the bid documents, vendors must meet certain specifications: Bibles must be the King James Version; must contain the Old and New Testaments; must include copies of the Pledge of Allegiance, Declaration of Independence, U.S. Constitution and the Bill of Rights; and must be bound in leather or leather-like material.

A salesperson at Mardel Christian & Education, a company that sells Christian products searched, and though they carry 2,900 different Bibles, none of them fit the parameters.

But one Bible fitted perfectly: Lee Greenwood's God Bless the U.S.A. Bible, endorsed by former President Donald Trump and commonly referred to as the Trump Bible, was the only bible in existence that fit all the parameters.

You could purchase an ordinary bible for $3. The Trump bible cost $60 each with The Tangerine Tantrum receiving fees for his endorsement.

Because that's what Jesus would have wanted.

Fun fact – the Superintendent wanted 55,000 bible, one for each classroom, but there's only 35,000 classrooms in the entire state.

In his latest financial disclosure, unearthed by woke lefty activists, Citizens for Responsibility and Ethics, Trump had received $300,000 in royalties so far for the God Bless America Bible.

Praise the Lord.

Back home, in revolving door news, it was discovered that over 100 people from the oil and gas sector had taken up senior government roles under the Conservatives, and two dozen had left such positions to work for major oil companies.

Since 2011, 127 former oil and gas employees in total – including 49 industry bosses or senior executives – had been recruited into top Tory government roles and ministerial advisory boards.

Almost three quarters worked for at least one of three major energy giants: BP, Shell or Centrica.

In their time in power, Conservatives had tended to be strongly against the phasing out of fossil fuels and were dead set against the Labour government's green agenda.

Hard to fathom how these coincidences keep happening.

A study by The Tax Justice Network showed that UK overseas territories including the British Virgin Islands made up the world's worst tax havens and were responsible for about £63bn in global tax avoidance.

They ranked countries on their involvement in helping multinational corporations underpay income tax in other countries.

The British Virgin Islands, Cayman Islands and Bermuda made up the top three. They are all UK overseas territories, for which the Westminster government has legal and constitutional responsibility.

Countries lose £63bn in corporate tax each year due to multinational corporations using the UK and its overseas tax havens, but it's worse than that, because when tax evasion from wealthy individuals is included, the amount rises to £126bn.

If corruption had a logo, it would the Union Flag.

Sue Gray had been lauded by MPs who fell over themselves to heap praise on her when she was appointed to investigate the various shenanigans of Boris "Mr Blobby" Johnson and his partying minions during lockdown.

A woman of unimpeachable credentials, a figure of integrity, rectitude and beyond reproach, they said.

She was later made Chief of Staff under Keir Starmer, and those that had praised her before, spun round so quick they almost screwed themselves into the ground.

As they had fulsomely admired her abilities and fairness, it would have been hard to claim that those qualities had somehow vanished, so a very great amount was made about her salary, which had exceeded the random metric of being greater than that of the Prime Minister.

There were 370 officials that earned more than S'Kier but the constant attention levelled at her forced the PM to bravely let her go, or she resigned to take the heat off the new government. Either way, Sue was out, eventually to find comfort in the world's most luxurious retirement home, the House of Lords.

In the outside world, millionaires were furious at the thought they might have to pay some tax.

Labour's budget plans to make the tax rules fairer were so unfair, said those that could afford to pay, but would prefer not to.

Charlie Mullins, a man who looked like a cross between a police sketch artist's Rod Stewart, crossed with a dental whitening advert, threatened to leave.

He went on daytime television to declare that he would rather not dip into his vast fortune and stay in clement London, the world's most exciting and diverse city, preferring instead to keep his money and relocate to Dubai, a place so hot you could burst into flames on leaving the airport, with decency laws from a previous millennium and the cultural attractions of a Butlin's holiday camp.

The plumber was not alone in threatening to leave. The super rich always do, whenever they are asked if they wouldn't mind contributing a bit to the country that enabled them to accumulate their wealth.

They told us they'd leave the last time there was a cut to non-doms' tax relief but just 5% of them did.

Still not missing them.

Conservative leadership hopeful Robert Jenrick was asked on LBC whether he regretted ordering cartoon characters to be removed from the walls of a children's asylum-seeker centre.

He explained that he was "very worried at the time and continue to be" about adults coming to the country illegally and posing as children.

He'd had a year to formulate his response and all he could come up with was that he was protecting us from adults pretending to be children.

How removing smiling Mickey Mouse cartoons from the wall of a reception centre would put off adults pretending to be children from pushing off from France in a dinghy to come here, he could not say, and hoped he would not be asked.

He said he regretted the decision and if he had his time over again, he might have acted differently.

From the looks of his bovver-boy haircut and malevolent demeanour, he would force children to wash the murals off with their own tears.

The Tories had whittled the list of potential leaders down to Jenrick and Badenoch.

Gruesome and gruesomer.

In the Scottish town of Elgin, residents were asked to report if dive-bombing seagulls were affecting their mental health.

NatureScot, the heritage body, reported that seagull populations were declining but residents begged to differ.

Pest controllers said the town was faced with 'epidemic' numbers during the breeding season.

Rob Teasdale, of Specialist Vermin Control, said: 'They are like the Luftwaffe the way they come off the roof and everyone dives for cover as they swoop at things.'

Worse - the Luftwaffe didn't poop on your car.

On the Isle of Man, a chip shop offered a £1 insurance policy offering a free meal if a feathered Messerschmitt stole your chips.

In Lancashire, locals spoke of apocalyptic swarms of 3,000 gulls made it difficult to go outside.

They remain a protected species, even though we need protection from them, not the other way round.

In the land of the Trumplethinskin, the Tangerine Scream had one of his safe-space rallies in Scranton, Pennsylvania.

A crowd behind him held signs aloft saying, "Scranton Firefighters for Trump", as he droned on about the "late great Hannibal Lector" and whether he would prefer to be electrocuted by a sinking boat's battery or eaten by a shark.

Alert members of the Scranton Fire Department firefighters' union noticed that they could not recognise any of those people with the signs.

Turns out they were not firefighters at all, just fans of Donny pretending to be.

Nothing to do with us, said Trump, when asked about this afterwards, a claim that would have sounded more believable had he not stated that, "We got the firefighters endorsed us, you probably heard", during the event.

He said, "That's a very good-looking group of human beings," which was also not true.

Back home Boris "Mr Blobby" Johnson was making a decent living scribbling foaming nonsense in a national newspaper.

"Labour looks venal and corrupt" read the headline of one of his columns.

No-one knows more about venality and corruption than Blobby.

He produced little vignettes on video to publicise these pieces that he posted on social media. They recorded his increasing dishevelment over the year, like a camera pointed at a wilting flower, for one of those time-lapse David Attenborough documentaries.

By the time this ridiculous piece hit the stands, he had come to resemble a ball of lard that had been rolled around a barber shop floor and left in a hedge overnight in a storm.

Bodge, like the rest of the Conservative Party, used to be close with various monied Russians but had made a point of distancing himself from them once the war in Ukraine broke out, adopting the mantle of the Putin Resistance.

Putin had not fared well in the war of late and had elicited the help of fellow murderous dictator Kim Jong Un of North Korea to bolster his troops of the front line.

Lil' Kim duly sent 12,000 callow conscripts who checked their phones on arrival in Russia and discovered a whole universe of pornography they had been denied in the Democratic People's Republic.

Battle hardened Ukrainians mowed them down in their thousands - from stiff to stiffs.

Putin, meanwhile, was seen continuously scratching his face and neck during televised appearances.

It was like he'd had tea with an opponent and forgotten which cup to drink from.

His health had been the subject of intense speculation for several years, and had been spotted coughing incessantly, his hands and feet making seemingly involuntary jerky movements like he was dancing sitting down, like exercise hour in an old peoples' home.

Whatever it was, it had not proved fatal so far, unfortunately.

The new Labour government pressed ahead with some of the old Conservative regime's plans for cuts to benefits and eligibility criteria.

This annoyed the Tories very much, even though it was their own idea.

What was to prove most eye-catching was the change in agricultural relief on inheritance tax.

People who were pretending to be farmers for the tax break had a fit you could see through a hay bale.

To say that the billionaire, off-shore, tax avoiding, non-dom media magnates who controlled the bulk of the British press were upset, would be an understatement.

They also happen to own a lot of agricultural land.

Could the two things possibly be connected?

While pretend farmers were worrying about the tax they might have to pay on the land they bought as a dodge, real farmers were concerned about the thing they needed more than anything else: water.

According to a report from the Global Commission on the Economics of Water, more than half the world's food production was at risk of failure within 25 years unless urgent action was taken to conserve water resources and end the destruction of the ecosystems on which our fresh water depends.

Half the world's population already faced water scarcity, and the climate crisis will just make that worse, they said.

But as they were experts with the evidence to back up their claims, no one was remotely interested in anything they had to say.

We're not interested in facts any more - we're all about feelings now, and we feel that if we ignore something, it will go away.

As much as humankind has a plan, that's it. What could possibly go wrong?

A senior Tesla executive quit with an attack on Europe's competitiveness after regulators put the brakes on Elon Musk's self-driving technology.

Marc Van Impe, Tesla's outgoing head of global vehicle automation and safety policy, said a crucial decision on rules governing how the system would work on British and European roads had been delayed, possibly until 2028.

If that's true then we had four short years to cross the road.

You should cross every road you're ever going to need to get to the other side of now, to avoid catastrophic injury later.

Musk rolled out Full Self-Driving software in the US in 2020 and it rolled out into traffic and caused a pile up you could see from one of his SpaceX rockets

According to iSeeCars, Tesla Model S and Model Y were two of the most dangerous cars on the road by occupant fatality rate.
A LendingTree survey found that Tesla cars had the worst accident rate in the US in 2023, with 24 accidents per 1,000 drivers.

A Washington Post analysis found that Tesla's Autopilot was involved in 736 crashes and 17 fatalities since 2019.

Apart from that, there's no reason why we shouldn't be giving Musk and Tesla permission to do anything they want on our roads, in case they lose profits because of an abundance of caution.

Let's not be mean. Billionaires aren't made of money, you know.

In Russia, there was a BRICS summit – that is, a summit featuring the countries that can't get an invite to other summits due to their behavioural issues - Brazil, Russia, India, China, South Africa, Iran, Egypt, Ethiopia, and the United Arab Emirates.

As Putin headed into his final press conference of the summit yesterday, he appeared in good spirits having enjoyed the attention of a largely captive audience, but he always has a captive audience, literally held captive until the Dear Leader decides to let them go.

His bonhomie evaporated as the BBC's Steve Rosenberg was granted the opportunity to ask the final question of the session.

Rosenberg put it to Putin that his war in Ukraine was in contravention of the tenets underpinning BRICS - that of justice, regional stability and security, and a fair world.

"How does this all match your actions of the past two and a half years? The invasion of Russian troops into Ukraine - where is the justice, stability and security?" he asked.

As Rosenberg delivered his line of questioning Putin was seen furiously scribbling on a notepad like a doctor scribbles on a prescription pad: "take one cup of polonium twice a day until all symptoms of life are gone".

Speaking of death, the government had proposed a ban on outside smoking at hospitality venues like pub gardens.

The Government was said to be spooked, however, by warnings from the hospitality industry that the measure could lead to job losses and pub closures.

Or, put another way, the brewing giants spent a ton of money on lobbyists who had ringing ministers' phones off the hook trying to get the smoking ban put out like the butt end of a fag.

Downing Street was subsequently reported to be blocking moves to include a ban on smoking outdoors in their Tobacco and Vapes bill amid fierce opposition by the hospitality trade and even fiercer opposition from cigarette companies, the world's most deadly drug dealers, who kill so many people that Mexican cocaine cartels seem like nursery school teachers by comparison.

In "fury as..." news, outrage erupted after the Royal British Legion announced they had a new pin for sale that paired the red poppy with the Progress Pride flag.

This was like the rainbow Pride flag but with more colours.

The right-wing press had a cow. They HATE colours.

The papers selected random members of the purple-faced public to comment on this, and to an old man they said it was "wokery gone mad".

That story again: poppy being sold as usual, with another one available should you want it, caused the permanently furious to blow their tops like they'd been asked to sit through Drag Queen Story Hour wearing suspenders and a tutu.

In Clacton news, Nigel Farage was representing it on the world stage by going to America to suck up to Donald Trump. Again.

He was not always in America, though. He also went to Malaysia to speak at an event called the Nomad Capitalist conference.

Since being elected in July, he had declared an income of £222,820.39 on top of the £91,000 plus expenses he got for working tirelessly, day and night as an MP.

What industry. An inspiration to us all.

November

Spain was hit by a new flooding disaster as torrential rain sent cars floating down the street in Girona.

Many ended up piled on top of each other by a bridge in front of the town casino, where you could go inside and bet on what was causing all this.

This happened just over a week after another flooding disaster hit Spain, in the Valencia region, with more than 200 people confirmed to have died, in scenes that looked like they came from a disaster film. But Bruce Willis would not be coming to save us.

Tons of mud and debris clogged street after street, filling thousands of ground floors, destroying living rooms and kitchens.

Whole neighbourhoods were left without shops and supermarkets after all their products were ruined. Many families did not have drinking water.

At every corner, cars are piled on top of one another or smashed into buildings, light poles, trees and bridge overpasses.

Meanwhile, the chief executive of the Cop29 climate conference was been filmed apparently agreeing to facilitate fossil fuel deals at the summit.

The Cop29 climate summit was held in Azerbaijan, with the aim of speeding up and paying for the shift to a clean economy.

Azerbaijan was known for two things: firstly, that no one knows how to spell it and second, its exports include and seem to be limited to oil and gas.

The world went to talk about reducing the reliance on fossil fuels in a country which counts 95% of the value of its exports as oil and gas.

No one cared about that, however, because...

Donald Trump won the U.S. Election but nobody cried that it was rigged, because the other side are grown-ups.

Perhaps too grown up. Elon Musk was said by close associate Seth Rogan to have had "an app" which told Musk the result of one of the closest elections in American history four hours before it was announced.

If the Democrats had won and their biggest donor had known that early, Trump would have been calling for an investigation in all caps and exclamation marks from now 'till the end of time.

Ordinary farmers were outraged that the Evil Socialist Labour Government was going to make them pay half the rate of inheritance tax after double the allowances that everyone else gets.

No farmer that is not a millionaire would be affected by the changes to inheritance tax but that did not stop non-millionaires coming out in force to protect the wealth of the landed gentry and the super-rich who had been buying up farmland as a tax dodge.

Nigel Farage appeared at a rally in spotless wellies, mustard corduroy trousers and a flat hat that he probably bought on Jermyn Street for as much as a cow would cost.

He showed up to an ecstatic reception from grinning men with wild hair who did not associate him with the Brexit that had decimated their livelihoods.

"No farmers, no food", read the banners, as though that was a killer argument to let a tiny number of the richest people in the land get away without paying what everyone else does.

You could say: no teachers, no progress; no nurses, no healing; no police, no security. None of that would wash as an excuse to pay no inheritance tax.

Why should landowners expect special treatment?

The answer to that question is that they expect it because they have always had it.

Fortunes have always been passed down the line of succession tax free, that's why the same families are still rich, decades or centuries after making their money.

That the poor have always stood up for this system is part of the British malaise – we love to be subservient to our "betters".

Positively insist on it, we do.

The Evil Socialist Labour Government was also addressing the weird system by which those not rich enough to send their children to private school were subsidising those that are.

VAT on private school fees was announced, and the refrain of "that's just the politics of envy" could be heard through the walls of a soundproofed room.

We will not be able to afford an extra 20%, wailed families from beyond the sweeping driveways and double doors of their detached houses.

They did not moan when the price of school fees had risen by 55% in ten years, they just paid up, because those fees weren't going to be spent on other people's children.

They would go to building a new swimming pool complex and a boating lake house for their own.

In other money news, the Chief Secretary to the Treasury claimed the UK was still suffering from the trauma of Liz Truss's economic mismanagement.

Darren Jones said "I think we've all got PTSD from Liz Truss,"

Close but not quite. We had PTLD: Post Traumatic Liz Disorder.

He said: "Under Liz Truss they sacked the permanent secretary [to the Treasury], they ignored the independent Office for Budget Responsibility, they announced £45bn of unfunded tax cuts and said they were only just getting started. And then the market went mad, and we all know what happened then."

Yes, a lettuce became the prime minister of this country by wining a game in The Star newspaper.

The Tangerine Scream got down to the serious business of picking the people who would run his government while he spent more time cheating at golf.

He selected the vaccine sceptic and partially brained Robert F Kennedy Jr as his health czar.

Trump gets the best people. Apart from those he selected the last time he was in the White House, all of whom were either in jail, just released or were busy calling him a Nazi and warning Americans not to vote for him.

Too late.

This time, his first pick was a man who says a worm ate some of his brain and who thinks childhood vaccines cause autism, that AIDS came from a vaccine, said Covid was designed to save Chinese and Jewish people, that school shootings are caused by antidepressants and that Wi-Fi causes your brain to leak.

Maybe he'd been sitting too close to his router.

Trump weighed all that up and said Robert F Kennedy Jr was "to take care of health", including "women's health".

A man who had been found liable of sexually abusing a woman in a store changing room was giving a man who had apologised for sexually assaulting a former family babysitter control over women's health.

Trump's cult fans were so thrilled they could barely shoot straight.

Back home, it wasn't much better. Two ex-leaders popped back up like bad smells you couldn't beat out of the rug.

The Blunder Truss and Mr Blobby had books they were keen to sell.

Liz's was called "I was right about everything", Bodger's was titled "Its all worse without me".

Something like that.

Labour continued upsetting all the right people, not just the right-wing people.

Ryanair's chief executive Michael O'Leary claimed Labour's decision to hike air passenger duty by 15% in the autumn Budget was idiotic.

The levy would increase by £2 to £15 for short-haul flights.

O'Leary said that the decision would cause him to cut capacity by 10% next year and would mean much more expensive travel for the ordinary traveller.

Such a lot of wailing for a £2 hike.
Do you know what you can buy for £2 on a Ryannair flight? Nothing.

As for £15, you couldn't get a bag in the hold for that, or one in the overhead locker either. Ryannai charged an extra £21 for a seat in the first five rows and £20 to issue a boarding card, but an extra £2 was going to ruin people's holidays?
Right.

In more confected furious farmer news, there was the Daily Telegraph's "Welliegate", in which the paper interviewed two farmers about the choice of footwear of a Labour politician.

Those farmers were reported to have been left "furious" at Labour's Environment Secretary Steve Reed over the choice of his wellington boots.

The Secretary of State for Environment, Food and Rural Affairs was pictured just three months afte he assumed his current role sporting a pair of £420 leather lined wellies, which were said to have been gifted to him by Waheed Alli.

To be clear, he didn't accept a contract for £180m for medical equipment he failed to provide and bought a yacht with the money, he didn't help a developer swerve a £45m tax bill, he didn't go on holiday while a deadly virus took hold and started killing people, no...he wore a comfortable pair of boots on a farm, and the right wing press had a cow.

One of the furious farmers said that anything above £100 in value was not suitable footwear for a farm, and that might have been relevant had the Secretary of State actually been farming, but he wasn't. He was visiting a farm and, from the extensive collection of one pair of wellies at his disposal, he decided to wear those.

The year was just getting silly now, a notion underlined by Kemi Badenoch who had been elected the leader of the Conservative Party and announced that it was time to get down to business.

The business of what was answered swiftly. It was the business of blaming Labour for everything that was wrong in the land and specifically pointing the finger at immigrants.

She also said that the Tories had emerged from the leadership race more united than ever!

The Tories that had been tearing chunks out of each other for months while its leaders had tried to attract the attention of the membership. That party was more united than ever?

She said that Labour had come unstuck in its first few months because they didn't have a plan. This had been the refrain from the entirety of the right-wing ever since they lost the election.

Those people who had the answer "you lost, get over it" to any discussion of why Brexit was a failure, were on an elongated screaming fit that would embarrass a newborn.

As for the plan, in its first few months in power, to address the bin fire the Conservatives had left of the country, Labour announced a green infrastructure fund, set up a British energy company to be run for the benefit of the nation, rather than the benefit of Tory donors, announced the renationalisation of the railways, gave local authorities control over local buses, introduced measures for free breakfast clubs in every primary school, liberalised the planning regime to get more housing built, improved workers rights, increased the minimum wage, scrapped the ruinously expensive gimmick of Rwanda, started to sort out the mess of the justice system left by the Tories, quelled the far-right riots, announced a big boost to the NHS, made the tax system fairer, made Jeremy Clarkson angry...I could go on...and what exactly had Kemi Badenoch done for the nation, apart from sow division, point the finger of blame at the poorest in society, and go on endless television programmes to bask in the glory that is herself?

And which of the remaining stars of the Tory party would be joining Badenoch as she chased Nigel Farage in a race to the bottom?

They used to call the most famous and long serving MPs the big beasts, but they didn't really have any of those left.

The remainder of the Tory party was just a selection of crackers like a tin of cheese biscuits.

James Cleverly, seen as the favourite for leader until his shock eviction in the final round of voting by MPs last month, announced he would not take a job in the shadow cabinet.

So we were going to be denied his cleverly-ness

Former Chancellor Jeremy Hunt also said he will not seek to serve.

He had decided to spend more time away from parliament, opening his eyelids so wide that they meet at the back of his head.

Ex-deputy PM Oliver Dowden was rumoured to be leaving the commons altogether, and the nation thought: which one's that?

Too late to become acquainted with him now.

The ex-Drear Leader, Tetchy Sunak insisted he would not leave Parliament, and that he would return to the backbenches.

Nobody believed that.

He was more likely to return to the back bench of one of his kitchens in one of his houses with a sea view in California.

Badenoch said in her victory speech, "I want to thank Rishi, no one could have worked harder in such difficult times"

Maybe she does have a sense of humour, after all.

As for the clapped out, empty shell that was Boris Johnson, he said Kemi would being "zing and zap" to the Tories, which was so very him, and a reminder why we don't ever want to see him again, or hear from him again ,or read his scribbled column or buy his book, mountains of which were still available in book shops everywhere.

Among the other "achievements" on his CV, Mr Blobby used to be our Foreign Secretary, a position gifted to him by Theresa May as what we assumed was some sort of in-joke.

The current head of the F.O. was David Lammy, who described his previous remarks about the US president-elect, Donald Trump, as "deluded, dishonest, xenophobic, narcissistic" and a "neo-Nazi-sympathising sociopath" as old news.

Old but also completely correct in every respect.

Keir Starmer's government was making efforts to smooth over tensions with the incoming president.

They would not have been wetting their pants if it had been Kamala Harris that had won.

They would not be haring round battening down the hatches from the in-coming storm if it had been a reasonable person who won the US election, but it wasn't, so now the government were freaking out because the American people decided that the terrible offspring of Back to the Future's baddie Biff Tanner and Cartman out of South Park should be their leader.

Lammy was pressed on his past critical comments but dismissed them, adding it would be a "struggle to find any politician" who had not said some "pretty ripe things" about Trump.

Asked if he apologised for remarks including calling the president-elect a "neo-Nazi-sympathising sociopath" or if Trump brought them up when they met in New York in September, Lammy said "not even vaguely".

He didn't have to. Vice-President elect and full-time eyeliner model JD Vance was on the attack for him.

Vance said. "I was talking with a friend recently and we were talking about, you know, one of the big dangers in the world, of course, is nuclear proliferation, though, of course, the Biden administration doesn't care about it.

"And I was talking about, you know, what is the first truly Islamist country that will get a nuclear weapon, and we were like, maybe it's Iran, you know, maybe Pakistan already kind of counts, and then we sort of finally decided maybe it's actually the UK, since Labour just took over."

In response, Deputy PM Angela Rayner said Vance had said "quite a lot of fruity things in the past".

And looked quite fruity while saying them, too.

With an eye on the Tangerine Tornado to come, Keir Starmer was warned that he must prioritise attempts to reset Britain's relationship with the EU and unpick the trade barriers created by leaving if he wanted to offset the impact of the tariffs Donald Trump had threatened to impose.

We had deliberately cut ourselves off from the gang we used to pall around with.

Now the school bully had ben released from borstal and he was back in the playground looking for someone to pick on.

Was he going to pick on a gang of 27 kids, or go after the single child who fell out with that gang and is now a sitting duck?

That is the level we exist at.

We adults aren't any different to kids, except kids aren't usually as filled with hate and greed, because they haven't lived long enough.

Trump had proposed a 10 per cent tariff on all US imports and a 60 per cent levy on Chinese-made products, which would affect the entire world's economy, but as Donny's world extends no further than the end of his own nose, he wasn't much interested in that.

Despite the assurances of Felonius Skunk, it is Americans who would pay his tariffs, not the countries that he would be slapping the tariffs on.

His cultists might notice eventually, but by the time they do, Donito will have told them it was Hilary's fault, or Joe Biden's, and they could protect themselves from those tariffs by buying a special edition Donald Trump bitcoin that has no value but does feature a super hero cartoon of him in a bathing suit.

Available now from Trump Enterprises.

After the budget, Stuart Rose, the former boss of Marks & Spencer and Topshop, who was running Asda, said the increase in employers' NICs and changes to tax thresholds would have "consequences" and meant it could not rule out some price increases.

Asda must have been only just scraping by, if a 77p per hour increase in the minimum wage was going to impact their business.

Poor Asda.

Rose added that the changes in the budget meant that Asda would "have to look hard at every piece of expenditure", including the annual pay increase for staff, and may limit how many workers it hires.

In other Asda news, from April of this year, profits at the UK's third-biggest supermarket chain grew 24% in 2023, topping more than £1bn in a year where non-CEO headed households struggled with the cost of living.

How would the company cope?

A new book by the chief architect of Project 2025, the policy plan for a second Trump term, repeatedly employed imagery of fire and burning, including calling for right-wingers to "burn away the rot" of American institutions and organizations deemed opposed to conservative aims.

Kevin Roberts, president of the far-right Heritage Foundation, advocated "a long, controlled burn" of targets including but not limited to…almost everything.

He wrote, "For America to flourish again, they don't need to be reformed; they need to be burned. A nice start would include: every Ivy League college, the FBI, the New York Times, the National Institute of Allergy and Infectious Diseases, the Department of Education, 80% of 'Catholic' higher education,, the Boy Scouts of America, the Bill and Melinda Gates Foundation, financial firm BlackRock, the World Economic Forum, the Chinese Communist Party, and the National Endowment for Democracy." and the Loudoun County Public School System (which in case you're wondering, wanted to change their name to one that doesn't celebrate slavery).

As for "every Ivy League college", those are the ones you've heard of: Harvard, Yale, Princeton etc. They're like America's Oxford and Cambridge universities.

Can you imagine a person being invited to write policy for the Prime Minister of this country saying we should burn down Oxford and Cambridge universities, even metaphorically speaking?

You'd think he was nuts.

And he even wants to destroy the Boy Scouts of America.

The kids with the toggles and the knots.

Worse for the incoming administration was the animus towards Blackrock, which had been a key investor in the Trump Media & Technology Group, and owned a large chunk of pretty much everything valuable on Earth.

Think of all the Bond villains rolled together and turned into a financial firm. That's Blackrock. They would probably have a solid gold extinguisher on hand to douse the flames of any pyromaniac who wanted to set fire to it.

Less controversially for the right wing of the right wing party, Roberts wanted political purges of the government and legal attacks on groups including women and gays and the whole LGBTQ+ community, because…of course he does.

The man who wrote the plan for Trump's second term in office wrote that fire is good, that there's plenty of fuel and that many of America's institutions serve only as shelter for our corrupt elite.

Corrupt elite!

What is it with these people and their phoney "war" on the elite?

If they aren't millionaires, they're billionaires and they're always going on about destroying the elite.

News flash - if you've got a small yacht to ferry you back and forth to your bigger yacht, you ARE the elite.

The Mayor of London, Sadiq Khan was accused of selling out, as Tube drivers were offered a four-day week, paid lunch breaks and an above-inflation pay rise to stop London Underground strikes.

The deal involved cutting drivers' working hours by 2.5 hours a week, putting them on a four-day, 35-hour week.

They would also get a 4.5 per cent pay increase and an extra week of extra paternity pay, whereas the press would have preferred something along the lines of the latter part of Monty Python's Yorkshiremen sketch, in which they should go to work for 34 hours a day AND pay t' mill owner for the privilege.

On the same day this story broke, the same newspapers were telling us of the gruelling week that City investment bankers worked.

Don't pity the poor bankers though, the papers said, because the starting salary was upwards of £170,000 per year.

The difference in attitude between train drivers being so greedy as to ask for a £63,000 salary and poor bankers and corporate lawyers struggling by on £170,000 was stark.

The bankers were worth it, because they were white collar workers, not some uppity working class oiks on the make.

To distract from all this, there were reports of an invasion of aliens from space.

The Pentagon released a report that revealed hundreds of documented incidents of unidentified and unexplained aerial phenomena (UAPs).

The Pentagon said they did not know what they were, which was not comforting.

The review detailed 757 cases of UAP encounters that were reported to US authorities over the past year or so.

They were reported by people who are not normally prone to flights of fancy, being as they were fliers of commercial and military aircraft as well as ground-based observers.

Of all the close encounters with mystery craft, no injuries or crashes were reported in any of the incidents.

Which means aliens are much better drivers that we are.

I mean, can you imagine how tired they would be after the flight to get here?

We humans feel destroyed after flying to another continent – they're coming from another galaxy.

Meanwhile, a whistleblower report on the US government's top-secret UFO data retrieval program revealed shocking evidence of Non-Human Intelligence (NHI) on Earth.

The report detailed the findings of an Unacknowledged Special Access Program (USAP) established to 'detect' and 'quarantine' the military's best UFO imagery, videos, eyewitness testimonies and electronic sensor evidence.

It featured numerous eyewitness accounts from 1991 through 2022, including flying metallic orbs, jellyfish-shaped aircraft, and UFOs that reportedly altered witnesses' perception of time.

The public-version of the report also discussed how infrared satellites captured footage of a massive

400-foot-wide saucer-shaped UFO soaring out of a dense cloud.

Don't be alarmed, but that's exactly how Independence Day started.

Donald Trump hosted a star-studded Mar-a-Lago bash where he announced a plan to start his presidency two months early.

The stars included and were limited to Sylvester Stallone, who looked like what would happen if you put a sausage in the microwave and forgot to prick its skin.

The president-elect and self-confessed world's leading genius introduced his selection to lead Health and Human Services.

Let me guess, cried Americans...Daffy Duck?

Was it Elmer Fudd?

No, worse – it was a tin foil hat conspiracy theorist who thinks a worm ate his brain.

Of Robert F. Kennedy Jnr., Trump said, "Today I nominated him for, I guess, if you like health and you like people that live a long time, it's the most important position."

Trump said he would let Kennedy 'go wild' on federal health agencies.

Trump said to Kennedy "I think you're going to do some unbelievable things"

That seemed quite likely, but not in a good way.

British experts and medics reacted with alarm to Kennedy's appointment.

Kier Starmer on the other hand, said that he looked forward to working with the president-elect on any bat-poop crazy notion that flits across his tangerine forehead because we in Brexit Britain were desperate and dateless, having divorced from the hottest partner round these parts.

As a sort of mid-life relationship crisis, Great Britain was dressing like we were yearning for love, showing WAY too much skin, posting selfies of ourselves and hoping that Donald Trump wouldn't swipe left.

Former Man United player Roy Keane shared his fury over the actions of his neighbours in Altrincham, Cheshire.

Reacting to what he thought was a red card incident, he said: "I took my dog out this morning at 7.15 where I live and someone is on the blower with the leaves at quarter past seven in the morning. It's a disgrace. I think it should be banned."

He went on to say: "I was gonna go over and say people are in bed! You're not allowed to use them. It's 8 o'clock."

I agree with Roy Keane, a sentence I am surprised to be writing.

He should have gone over.

Can you imagine having Roy Keene yelling at you over the noise of your leaf blower?

You'd gulp so hard you'd swallow your face.

Car company Jaguar released an advert that caused the Purple Faced Fury Brigade to have a fit you could hear from the bottom of the Mariana Trench.

It featured eccentrically dressed models of various degrees of wokeness and inclusion.

Apart from that technicolour shock, the company also unveiled a new logo, ditching the "growler" big cat's face that had adorned the bonnets of all of the cars driven by criminals in The Sweeney.

The "car" they chose to feature appeared to have been stolen from Lady Penelope out of The Thunderbirds.

It wasn't a real car, it was one of those mock-ups that car firms use to get publicity, like fashion houses send models down runways wearing a flowerpot on their heads with their feet slipped into two hamsters. That stuff is not for sale, it's for attention.

And Jaguar certainly got a lot of attention.

The CEO explained that they wanted to appeal to un-stereotypical Jag owners, because if they kept relying on people who look like Nigel Farage to buy their models, they'd be out of business by next week.

Nonsense, said the fact-averse.

Our sales are a third of what they were five years ago, said the numbers.

The outrage was short lived because Boots released their Christmas advert, which featured non-white people, and the easily incensed ran off to shout about that instead.

December

Greece was hit hard by Storm Bora, with torrential rain, gale-force winds and intense thunderstorms affecting the islands of Rhodes and Lemnos.

Meanwhile, Australia had an unusually wet start to its summer. Severe thunderstorms swept across the eastern regions, bringing heavy rainfall – more than 100mm in some areas – and large hailstones in Sydney, Brisbane and Victoria.

In South America, severe thunderstorms affected Brazil, Argentina and Uruguay and in this country, the Met Office issued a rare red "danger to life" warning as Storm Darragh swept in, but no-one had any time for that because...

London Mayor Sadiq Khan was set to receive a knighthood.

The massed ranks of foamers all yelled "What for?", at the same time.

Those people that were perfectly OK with son of ex-KGB agent Evgeny Lebedev being elevated by Boris Johnson to become Baron Lebedev of Siberia (!) and sit in the House of Lords for the rest of his life and said nothing while the same Bodger Johnson gave his brother a peerage and were silent when Mr Blobby placed Charlotte Owen, whoever she is, in the upper chamber, having done nothing of note in her short life, were incensed that a thrice elected Mayor of London was to be recognised for an honour.

Priceless.

After a year of negative publicity, abysmal behaviour and being shamed on a daily basis by Feargal Sharkey, Britain's water companies apologised and offered their customers compensation for their failings.

Just kidding, they said they wanted to see higher returns for their shareholders, so that they could begin the investment in the infrastructure that we thought we had been paying for since they were given away for pennies by Margaret Thatcher's government 35 years ago.

Stuart Colville, the deputy chief executive of the industry body Water UK, said shareholders were not receiving enough.

Since privatisation, the water companies had borrowed £85 billion and awarded themselves £73 billion of that for excellence in being them.

The companies explained to the regulator that they needed to raise water bills by £144 over the next five years in order to give themselves more money.

The regulator put its foot down and said they could raise them by £94.

I'm no expert on negotiation, but I suspect that if the companies wanted £94, they would ask for £144, expecting to be offered what they wanted, allowing the regulator to appear as though they were doing something on our behalf, rather than on behalf of the Chinese, American, Malaysian, German, Kuwaiti, Australian, and UAE wealth funds and financiers who own our water.

The companies claimed to be desperate to spend £104.5 billion on upgrading the infrastructure they should have been fixing all along.

That seemed like a weirdly precise number. £104.5, not 104.6 and definitely not 104.4.

It gave it the ring of authenticity, as though they had calculated precisely how much they would need, rather than just thought up a number and wrote it on a napkin.

The Tory supporting press claimed to be furious that Labour was "operating government by talking shop".

They fumed that Starmer had launched at least 67 reviews in the first five months they had been in office.

A reasonable response might have been: reviews are like looking both ways before you cross the road. It is good to know the state of things before committing yourself, and Labour had been out of power for 14 years, so reviews were necessary and not a waste of time.

But Labour did not say that. Instead, a Labour official hit back, telling Politico: "The Tories did about 61 reviews alone on whether to ban plastic cutlery — and got countless glowing Mail front pages as a result."

A very brief period of silence from that paper followed.

Here's a short list of the full blown pieces of legislation that Labour had passed or begun the process of parliamentary scrutiny since they won the election in July:

Budget Responsibility Act, Passenger Railway Services (Public Ownership) Act, Great British Energy Bill, Employment Rights Bill, Renters' Rights Bill, House of Lords (Hereditary Peers) Bill, Finance Bill, Tobacco and Vapes Bill, Data (Use and Access) Bill, Terrorism (Protection of Premises) Bill, Property (Digital Assets) Bill, Armed Forces Commissioner Bill, Financial Assistance to Ukraine Bill, Mental Health Bill, The Product Regulation and Metrology Bill and the Football Governance Bill.

In addition, they had introduced policies like:

Plan to end new HIV cases in England by 2030
Major reforms to the bus transport sector including allowing local authorities to set up publicly-owned bus companies
New funding for hundreds of school breakfast clubs ahead of an England-wide rollout next year
A new nuclear service commemoration medal for wronged British veterans

Ex-servicemen and women able to use veterans cards as voter ID
Single-use vapes to be banned from June 1st 2025
De facto ban on onshore wind farms had been lifted
New code of practice introduced for student accommodation landlords
Seafarers' Wages overhaul implemented, ensuring seafarers are paid the legal National Living Wage
New right for English councils to auction leases of vacant high street shops
Bibby Stockholm refugee detention barge closed
£700m Rwanda deportation scheme ended
Actions to address the prison overpopulation crisis
New compensation fund established for Infected Blood scandal victims
Ban implemented on hospitality employers taking staff tips
New sanctions introduced on Russia, Iran and Syria
Funding restored to United Nations Relief and Works Agency for Palestine Refugees
Largest-ever funding round for new renewable energy schemes to feed into the grid
National Energy System Operator nationalised
Expanded access to anti-overdose medications like naloxone
A new 'Fair Payment Code' to address late payments hitting small and medium businesses and sole traders

And they had reached pay deals, settling strikes with: teachers, health service workers and railway workers.

But apart from that, yes, they were all talk.

Local councils were certainly not all talk. They were serious about correcting people's behaviour and had the means to do it.

On-the-spot penalties issued for offences including but not limited to swearing, shouting, idling, loitering and begging, known as "busybody" fines, jumped 42% in 2023, according to a report.

The majority of the 19,162 penalties in England and Wales were issued by private enforcement companies which were paid according the number of fines they issued.

What could possibly go wrong?

The Manifesto Club report into breaches of public spaces protection orders found the highest issuing councils were Harrow, Redbridge and Hillingdon.

Harrow issued 3,919 penalties, with fines for amplification, feeding the birds, failing to produce a dog fouling bag, drinking and handing out leaflets.

Redbridge issued 3,550 penalties, including 3,016 for spitting, 142 for drinking alcohol in public, eight for leaflet distribution and three for gambling.

Hillingdon issued 3,060 penalties, including 2,335 penalties for "idling" (leaving the engine running for more than two minutes), 342 for spitting and 115 for motorised electric vehicles.

The report highlighted the case of a musician, David Fisher, who was fined for busking outside a Bruce Springsteen concert.

How could anyone hear him?

Most entertainingly, a Colchester cyclist was fined for locking his bike to a bike rack.

Donald Trump set about picking his cabinet.

With all the billionaires and multimillionaires that had been assembled by Trump, there was enough moral holes to fill the Albert Hall.

The mega-rich backers he chose for key positions had stated their aim to cut spending on public services that are used by the most poor and vulnerable.

In other words, the ding-a-lings that voted for the Tangerine Scream were going to be the first ones hurt by him.

At least 11 picks for strategic positions were billionaires, or married someone who was.

And if the drooling hicks think that their own interests and the interests of billionaires coincide, then I have a genuine non-existent picture of Donald Trump drawn as a super hero I would like to sell them, except they already bought one, yours for only $100 from Trump Enterprises, from which you can also buy Trump's signature fragrance, called "Fight, Fight, Fight", after the line he delivered when he got his ear nicked.

What does the great aroma of Donny actually smell like? In real life, according to former Republican Representative Adam Kinzinger, it was "armpits, ketchup, makeup and a little butt".

Splash it all over.

The richest of them all, Sissy Space-X, Elon Musk pledged to cut $2trillion from the national budget. He did not explained how or over what period, but he did warn that it may entail "temporary economic hardships".

So to be clear, the richest man the world has ever seen, who spent a quarter of a billion dollars on getting Trump elected, and whose fortune increased by $50 billion since the election was telling the poorest Americans that because of the things he was about to do to them, they were going to have to suffer financially.

In this country, we weren't doing much better.

Farmers were protesting about the inheritance tax rises that they weren't going to be affected by. They blocked roads which prevented ambulances from getting to A&E.

When anti-fossil fuel campaigners merely talked about protesting, it resulted in long prison sentences for them but the farmers suffered absolutely no consequences. In fact, they were supported in their disruption by the same Tory MPs and right-wing rags that condemned the fossil fuel protesters for doing the exact same thing.

The difference being that the anti-fossil fuel people were protesting on behalf of humankind. The farmers were protesting on behalf of their own kind.

There was also an online petition to have another election, just six months into a five year term of government. This was eagerly signed by the same people who had spent the past six years replying to every piece of Brexit bad news by repeating "you lost, get over it".

They had lost and they weren't getting over it at all.

Added to that, Elon Musk seemed to be having a very public breakdown which involved trolling whole countries, especially ours.

To top it all, multiple unexplained drone sightings were still being reported in the skies above New Jersey and subsequently elsewhere in America, Germany and Great Britain.

The Pentagon and the FBI claimed they did not know what they were, which was not comforting.

Either they did know and didn't want us to know, or they really didn't have a clue. Hard to know which would be worse.

In the midst of this, Kemi Badenoch went to war with lunch.

She channelled her inner Gordon Gekko by saying that lunch is for wimps, quoting the criminal fraudster and all-round person of evil intent from the film Wall Street.

She also said that sandwiches, the nation's favourite lunchtime fare, was "not real food", which is true in the same sense as the Tories are not a real party. Not a serious one, anyway. Not any more.

The sandwich issue sucked up so much oxygen that almost no-one noticed a report which revealed that because of stagnating wages, we Brits were £10,000 worse off every year.

Had earnings grown at the speed seen before the 2008 financial crash, the average adult would now be taking home more than £42,300 before tax.

In reality, median earnings in 2024 were £31,600.

But wealth had been created, so where had it gone?

Well, since the pandemic, the wealth of the five richest people in the world had doubled.

They were $3.3 trillion richer, their fortunes rising by twice as much as the rest of the world put together.

Meanwhile, the off-shore, foreign billionaire owned press were encouraging us to believe that striking nurses and demanding teachers were being greedy.

Never mind, NASA scientists warned that on Christmas Eve a massive 'asteroid' the size of a 10-story building would smash into Earth at 14,743mph.

They didn't – they said that on Christmas Eve a massive 'asteroid' the size of a 10-story building would skim *past* Earth at 14,743mph.

Asteroid 2024 XN1 would pass by harmlessly at a distance of 4.48 million miles from Earth, they assured us, and it did.

Space missed again.

It will get us one day, though.

Maybe next year.

Here's the A-Z of the year, as compiled with the help of listeners to my Christmas shows on LBC.

Thank you, if you helped. Thank you if you listened. Thank you for reading.

This year, a small change: no deaths.

A
Storm Ashley
Prince Andrew
Artificial Intelligence

Astronauts stranded on the ISS
Julian Assange freed
Ancient Rome: Trump says US and Italy allies since
Afghanistan: Taliban bans women from public spaces
Dianne Abbott, whip restored, re-elected
Albania bans TikTok
Lord Ali funds Starmer makeover
ABBA knighted in Sweden
American Riviera Orchard, Meghan's lifestyle brand
American tourist fined for stripping, Sangster Airport
Argentina win Copa America for record 16th time
Assad's rule in Syria ends
Lee Anderson defects to Reform UK
Anticyclonic gloom, persistent cloudy, dull weather
American election
Assisted Dying Bill
Alpaca sneezes on King Charles
Atlantic Meridional Overturning Circulation collapse warning
ATACMS, Biden OKs Ukrainian use of missiles on Russia
Alphabet, earliest known found in Syria
AfD, Musk endorses German extremist party
Ruben Amorim appointed manager of Manchester United
A23a, world's largest iceberg breaks free
Auroras seen in southern England
Azerbaijan, fossil fuel state hosts COP29
Phin "Barmy Brunch" Adams, baked bean balaclava
Al Jazeera banned in Israel
Francesca Albanese, UN, accuses Israel of genocide
Apple Intelligence launched
Agentic AI, autonomous, self learning
Ankara terrorist attack
Azerbaijan airline crash, Russia accused, Putin apologises
"APT" by Rosé and Bruno Mars tops world chart for 9 weeks
Anthony Ammirati, Olympic pole vaulter's pole goes viral
Australia announces social media ban on under-16s

B
Storm Burt
Bullseye returns to TV
Bricks: Southport protester hit in head and groin by own side
Baltimore bridge collapses after ship crash
Black hole in nation's finances
Burt, star of Crocodile Dundee dies
Boeing, planes grounded, Starliner fails
Beyoncé's country album
Steve Bannon, Trump ally jailed
Bambi Thug upsets some at Eurovision
Bibby Stockholm migrant barge closed
Baby Reindeer
Badger cull end announced
Bitcoin hits $100,000 value
Beau Lucy, escaped cow hit by police car

Band Aid 40, new version of song
Mr Bates vs the Post Office, TV docudrama
Brat summer, Charli XCX inspires trend
Brexit, still giving
Michel Barnier, PM of France, September to December
Banana and duct tape artwork sells for $6.2m
Rue David Bowie named in Paris
Kemi Badenoch named new Tory leader
Bovaer, anti-methane cattle feed additive
Breakaway bar discontinued by Nestle
Beards, Army lifts ban
Boring Phone launched
Bleach blonde bad built butch body: Jasmine Crockett to MTG
BT Tower sold to hotel group
Blackpool rock seeks protected status from Chinese imports
Breakdancing introduced to Olympics
Joe Biden bows out of presidential race
Joe Biden pardons son Hunter
Bromley FC promoted to EFL, becomes only stadium in Tory seat
Brazil bans X, then lifts ban after $5m fine paid
Balloons filled with rubbish sent by North Korea to South Korea
Bend, Oregon, googly eyes stuck on public sculptures
Bat shed for HS2
Bonds, Australian co. uses bearded non-binary bikini model
Butler, PA, scene of Trump shooting
Brain rot, word of the year, OED
Bayesian, yacht sinks mysteriously, kills 7
Brussels sprouts 20% bigger due to weather
Bluesky, Twitter alternative grows
Baby lotion, 1000 bottles at Sean "Diddy" Combs place
Hurricane Beryl, supercharged by ocean temperatures
Christoph Baumgartner, Austria, fastest goal in international football: 6s
Boots Xmas ad, boycott call due to black actors
BYD, Chinese electric car maker overtakes Tesla revenue
Simone Biles, US gymnast Olympics comeback
Steve Bray, longstanding protester ruins Sunak's election announcement
Bulgaria joins EU Schengen Area
Bobbing, Diane Abbott fails to attract Speaker's attention, PMQs
Bank account checks on DWP benefit recipients announced
Bank notes featuring Charles enter circulation
"Brexit means Brexit", joke kids say while tackling player not ball
Bottle caps attached, EU rule applies in UK despite "sovereignty"
David Blunkett falls into gap on Tube platform
Bes-mugs, psychedelics found in 2000 year Egyptian old cups
Body cams issued to retail staff after customer violence
Bishop of Newcastle v Archbishop of York re. sex scandal
Peter Bone MP, suspended, recalled
Barbie doll lookalike given to Camilla
Boogie bin, interactive bin introduced, Cirencester

C
Storm Conall
Climate change, 2024 hottest year on record
David Cameron, briefly Foreign Sec
Bill Clinton admitted to hospital
Cheddar cheese heist worth £300k from Neil's Yard Dairy
Cilla, wins National Cat Award
Cloud seeding in Dubai blamed for floods by climate change deniers
Church of England abuse scandal
Archbishop of Canterbury resigned
King Charles cancer treatment
King Charles found to be charging NHS rent for ambulance parking
Princess Catherine cancer treatment
Chagos Islands, UK negotiates to relinquish sovereignty
King Conker, David Jakins, cleared of cheating at world championship
Churchill's false teeth bough for £18,000
Churchill photo stolen in Canada found in Italy
Cadbury loses royal warrant
Cadbury turns 200
Cecil, dog eats $4000 cash owners had left out
Russ Cook becomes first to run length of Africa
Co-op Live arena finally opens after delays, Manchester
Cryptosporidium outbreak, South west Water
Corey Comperatore killed as bullet misses Trump, Butler PA
Clacton decides on Farage as MP
Clacton surprised at Farage absence
The Cure's comeback album well received
CrowdStrike IT outage causes 8.5m computers to crash
Copilot AI, Microsoft chatbot taunts those considering suicide
Chang'e-6, Chinese probe returns with dark side of Moon rocks
Radio Caroline turns 60
Naomi Campbell banned from being charity trustee
Coachella, Trump buses in fans to rally, then strands them
Jimmy Carter turns 100, longest living former president
Cinnamon the capybara escapes Shropshire zoo
Ethan Crumbley's parents found guilty re. his school shooting, Michigan
Sean "Diddy" Combs sexual assault allegations
David Coote, football referee sacked by PGMOL
Sam Carling, 22, becomes youngest MP
Cambridge Uni pro-Gaza protesters blank Suella Braverman
Chequers estate gate crashed into by drink driver Matthew Wootten
Jeremy Corbyn elected as independent MP
Mark Cavendish retires from cycling
E. Jean Carroll awarded $83.3m in damages against Trump
Magnus Carlson, world chess No.1 quits after told to change jeans
Culture wars
Coal-fired power plant, last one closed in UK
Cancer, mRNA vaccine trials

D

Storm Darragh emergency signal sent to 3m mobiles
Drones, UFO mass sightings
DOGE – US govt. efficiency dept. named after Musk hyped cryptocurrency
Dark matter, scientists say it links to a fifth dimension
Celine Dion performance Paris Olympics
Drowning Street, Sunak gets soaked announcing election
Ellen DeGeneres quits USA for UK
D-Day commemorations, Sunak leaves early
Dartmoor Prison evacuated over radon gas scare
Disfrutar, Barcelona: "World's best restaurant"
Dorchester Village, campaign to change name to Pooh Village
Yusuf Dikec, casual Olympic shooter goes viral
Dynamic pricing, excuse for ramping up ticket costs
Gaie Delap, 77, protester locked up at Xmas, wrists too small for tag
Difficult decisions: Starmer refrain
D:Ream blares out as Sunak announces election in rain
DragonFire laser, first high-power firing against aerial target
Charlotte Dujardin, dressage champion suspended for whipping
Drones as war weapons
Deadpool & Wolverine, highest grossing non-animated film of year
Diamond battery with 1,000 year lifespan unveiled
Devon cryptosporidium outbreak, South West Water
Daisy, AI "granny" designed to waste scammers' time
Armand Duplantis, pole vault, Olympic gold, BBC World Sport Star of Year
Disney settles Trump defamation suit over ABC News
Ed Davey's election campaign stunts
Anna Donelli, nun alleged to be conduit between mafia and prisoners, Italy
"Double fisted", Met Office warning of snow and ice
"Deny, defend, depose" written on shell casings, Luigi Mangione
"Delay, deny, depose, you people are next", Briana Boston arrested
Gukesh Dommaraju, 18, youngest ever world chess champion
Disney says man can't sue re. death of wife due to terms of Disney+ trial

E
ECHR: right-wingers want to leave
Eras Tour – Taylor Swift's record breaking concerts
Elections, more people voted worldwide than any other year
Euro 2024, England runners-up
E. coli in water supply
Endurance, Shackleton's ship 3D scanned
England football shirt flag colour row
Eiffel Tower model, world's largest matchstick creation, 23ft
Early release scheme to tackle prison overcrowding
Employment Rights Bill introduced
Egg and spoon race record – 2,700 competitors, Mexico
Elgin Marbles, row still ongoing
Extinction Rebellion
Marlene Englehorn, BASF heiress gives away 25m Euro fortune
The Evening Standard rebrands as The London Standard, goes weekly
Baltasar Ebang Engonga, Equatorial Guinea official makes 400 sex tapes
Election date gambling, 7 Met police officers investigated

Mount Everest found to be growing by 2 millimetres per year
Hugh Edwards, suspended sentence for indecent child images

F
Nigel Farage wins seat at 8th time of trying
Nigel Farage seldom seen in Clacton
"Farage riots" trends online after Southport unrest
Freak Off parties, Sean Combs allegations
Farmers protest at paying half the tax the rest of us pay
Figurative cave art, oldest discovered, Sulawesi, 51,200 years old
Fight, fight, fight: Trump's refrain after shooting
Fight, Fight, Fight: name of Trump's new perfume, $199
Fossil fuels
Filton 10 destroy Israeli bound weapons, Elbit Systems, Bristol
Flag Football introduced at Olympics
Fixing the foundations: Starmer refrain
Freebies, Starmer accused by Tories, kettle/pot
FIFA announce Saudi Arabia to hold World Cup 2034
Mark Francois appointed Shadow Minister for Defence!
Florida condos sinking, Miami
Forest fires found to be getting worse
Finland, still No.1: World Happiness Report
Nigel Farage attacked with milkshake by Victoria Thomas Bowen
Francis Scott Key Bridge collapses after ship crash, Baltimore
Nigel Farage replaces Richard Tice as leader Reform UK
Fen raft spiders released by Chester Zoo to halt decline
Far-right riots counter protests
"Forever chemicals" added to the Oxford English Dictionary
Fire station burns down Stadtallendorf, Germany

G
Glasses-gate, (Starmer) Tories try to distract from own corruption
Gaza
Elliot Giles breaks men's road mile world record, time 3:51.3
Rachael "Raygun" Gunn breakdances to infamy, Olympics
God Bless the USA Bible, Trump's version
Gambling, Sunak's staff bet on election date set by Sunak
Sue Gray – Tories' darling 'till she took up Labour post
George Galloway briefly an MP for Rochdale
Global warming, above 1.5C on pre-industrial level
Greece, first Christian Orthodox nation to legalise same-sex marriage
The Grand Tour, final episode
Michael Gove loses seat
Matt Gaetz, Trump's pick for AJ, ethics report
Willis Gibson beats Tetris in world first on live stream
Tom Gilbey taste tests 25 wines during London Marathon
General election
Great British Railways, state-owned operator announced
Guinness shortage
Garrick Club, old men's club admits women members
Grindavik volcano erupts, Iceland
Ghost orchid, ultra rare rediscovery, UK

Greenland, Trump demands purchase by USA
Greenland not for sale say Denmark, counter offer to buy USA
Global Legal Action Network challenges UK arms sales to Israel
Guilty, Trump, 34 felony counts
Gemini 2.0 AI assistant released by Google
Le Gavroche, restaurant closes after 56 years
Go-op, co-operatively owned rail operator approved
Gout Gout, Australian sprinter, 16, breaks U18 100m world record
Growth: Labour government refrain
Gary, 8ft gorilla statue stolen/found in lay-by, Dundee
Greenhouse gas emissions down 8% in EU, year on year
Gateshead Highway, flyover closed due to safety concerns
Georgia elections fraud allegations
German Navy boat plays Darth Vader theme on Thames

H
Hurricane Hugo
Hurricane Helene
Human rights, right-wing object
Hezbollah
Hamas
Houthis
Hanukkah and Christmas coincide in rarity
Kamala Harris
Hulk Hogan rips shirt off at Trump rally
Harrods, Al Fayed abuse allegations
Hawk Tuah girl goes viral
Haggis, newborn endangered pygmy hippo, Edinburgh Zoo
Hunting Kind, fox hunting group says they should be a protected minority
Hedgehog baby rescued, found to be hat bobble, Cheshire
Hyperia, UK's fastest roller coaster opens/shuts after one day
Frank Hester, Tory donor says MP Dianne Abbott "should be shot"
Hanbury, London Zoo penguin named after PR agency
Hippos can fly, found to have all 4 feet off ground at speed
Hush money, Trump
Duke Henry of Luxembourg announces abdication
H5N1 bird flu virus detected in US milk supply
HARDtalk axed by BBC after 25 years
Haka by Maori MPs suspends NZ parliament
Holiday Inn/Express housing migrants set on fire by far-right rioters
Honshu, Japanese macaque escapes Highland Wildlife Park
Horses from Household Cavalry, spooked, run through London
Lewis Hamilton announces move from Mercedes to Ferrari
Pete Hegseth, TV host named as defence chief by Trump
Halloween body bag decorations at soft play centre, Glos.
Anne Hughes, 72, caught in shop shutters goes viral
HMRC says you can pronounce H "aitch" or "haitch"
Homeless' tents cleared unlawfully admit Met Police
H-1B visas, Trump and Musk v. MAGA fans over immigration
Tom Hayhoe appointed Covid corruption commissioner
Halloween parade hoax, Dublin

I

Inheritance tax protests by farmers/landowners
Israel
ICC issues arrest warrants for Israeli leaders
Inside Out 2 becomes highest grossing animated film
Iran launches drone attacks against Israel
Immigration
Andrew Irvine remains found after 100 years, Everest
ISS astronauts stranded
Ichthyotitan jawbone, largest marine reptile, found, Somerset
IndiGo, airline lets women choose seat next to other women
Independent MPs – 5 elected
i360, Brighton attraction goes into administration

J

Robert Jenrick's campaign hats say "We want Bobby J": rude slang
Just Stop Oil protesters jailed
Japan Airlines plane crashes into coastguard aircraft, Tokyo
Al Jazeera banned in Israel
Jay-Z sexual assault allegations
Jaguar changes logo, releases advert that upsets foamers
Andrea Jenkyns defects from Tories to Reform
Boris Johnson turned away from polling station for lack of ID
Junior doctors should feel valued by smiles, not pay: Edwina Currie
Jet2 passenger Lily Ifield removed on refusing to pay £9 for sandwich
Jamaica tables bill to remove King Charles as head of state
Jubilee of Hope, Pope opens doors to inaugurate 2025 Holy Year
Jermaine Jenas sacked by BBC after complaints
Jewellery worth £10.4m stolen, one of UK's biggest burglaries

K

Korean (North) troops sent to fight for Putin
Joost Klein, Netherlands entrant disqualified from Eurovision
"Kiss my ass", Marjorie Taylor Greene to Foreign Sec. David Cameron
Kilauea volcano erupts, Hawaii
Jürgen Klopp leaves Liverpool FC
Herbert Kickl, Austrian far-right leader of FPO wins election
Dieter Klofkorn, set fire to US election ballots, says "not politically motivated"
Robert F. Kennedy Jr, anti-vaxxer picked as health sec. by Trump
K-pop act Seventeen plays Glastonbury
Gustav Klimt portrait found after 100 years
Kensington Palace releases doctored photo of Kate and children
Kneecap, Irish rappers win case against Badenoch for withholding arts grant
Kevin the Great Dane named world's largest dog, Iowa
Sadiq Khan, London Mayor knighted
Korea (South), martial law briefly declared
Kentucky man declared brain dead wakes during organ harvesting
Travis Kelce, Kansas City Chiefs, Taylor Swift's boyfriend

L

Storm Lilian
Little Shrew, Kate Bush animated film
Kendrick Lamar/Drake feud
Hannibal Lecter, "the late great": Trump at rallies
Lebanon
Lula da Silva, Brazilian president undergoes brain surgery
Gary Lineker announces departure from Match of the Day
Lyle's Golden Syrup logo rebrand after 150 years
Labour landslide at general election
Labour suspends 7 MPs over 2 child benefit cap rebellion
"Lunch is for wimps": Kemi Badenoch
LignoStat, first satellite made of wood launched
Laos, methanol in alcohol poisonings
London Overground rebranded

M

Meghan Markle, everything is her fault
Luigi Mangione shoots health insurance CEO
Luigi Mangione becomes internet folk hero
Elon Musk wins US election by spending $277 million
Elon Musk's wealth increases by $200 billion
Manchester City FC's results tank
MOD buys back 36,000 military homes for £6bn
Mary Donaldson, first Australian-born queen consort in world, Denmark
Medallia, Pip Hare's boat dismasted, Vende Globe race
Maggie, penguin renamed Magnus after misgendering, Birdland Park, Glos.
Massaco Tribe, 1st pictures of uncontacted people
Barry Manilow plays last UK dates
Morrissey can't find label to release new album
Mammoth baby's remains discovered, 50,000 years old, Siberia
Paul McCartney's Hofner bass guitar stolen 51 years ago, returned
"Mini moon" asteroid heads off into space
Davina McCall, TV presenter has brain op
Magdeburg Xmas market attack
Mannheim stabbing attack
Rupert Murdoch loses "Succession" battle with children
Richard Medhurst, journalist arrested using anti-terror legislation
Peter Mandelson named US Ambassador
Peter Mandelson called "moron" by Trump ally
Menendez brothers re-sentencing move after TV drama
Maternity pay "excessive": Kemi Badenoch
Mark Menzies, Tory MP quits amid party funds scandal
Paul McCartney becomes first UK billionaire musician
Andy Murray retires from playing tennis
Muslim Pride event, UK first
Penny Mordaunt: "Stand up and fight!"
Chris McCausland, blind contestant wins Strictly Come Dancing
Narges Mohammadi awarded the 2023 Nobel Peace Prize
Queen Margrethe II of Denmark abdicates
"My dad was a toolmaker": Starmer refrain

Craig Mackinlay, "bionic MP" returns to Parliament
"Manifest" named Cambridge Dictionary's 2024 word of the year
Moo Deng, baby hippo draws crowds, Thailand zoo

N
Benjamin Netanyahu, ICC arrest warrant
NASA Backyard project finds object moving at one million mph
Nobel Prize for Chemistry awarded to three AI pioneers
The National Lottery changes hands
NexusWave by Inmarsat launched to counter Musk's Starlink
National Insurance rise for employers announced
Rafael Nadal retires
Notre Dame reopens
Neuralink, Elon Musk's chip implanted in patient's brain
Northern Lights visible in southern England
"Never knowingly undersold", John Lewis promise returns
Nans against Nazis: pensioner's response to far-right rioters
Neonicotinoids, bee killing pesticide ban announced in UK
Nusantara replaces Jakarta as Indonesian capital
Alexei Navalny, Russian anti-corruption lawyer dies in prison
National service proposed by Sunak during election campaign
Nordic countries advise citizens on war preparations

O
Olympics opening ceremony upsets some
Ofwat, water regulator continues to be useless
Ofgem, energy regulator continues to be useless
Oasis announce comeback tour
Oasis ticket fiasco
OpenAI's Sora video generator released
Ozempic diabetes/weight loss drug
OnlyFans, Olympians' funding sideline
James O'Brien's LBC handover take-down of Farage in same studio
OceanGate Titan submarine hearing
Ofsted one word school rank removed
Bisan Owda, Palestinian journalist, wins Emmy
George Osborne calls Rachel Reeves his mini-me after cuts announced
Orca Tahlequah who carried dead calf gives birth again
Odyssey cruise ship stranded in Belfast for 4 months
Michelle O'Neill, first Irish nationalist First Minister
Orange powder paint thrown on Stonehenge by Just Stop Oil
Oxford-Cambridge Boat Race, rowers' illness due to E. coli
Observer, founded 1791, sold to Tortoise Media

P
Parker Solar Probe makes closest ever approach to the Sun
Pets, "they're eating the pets": Trump on Springfield residents
Pagers explode, Lebanon and Syria
Pret a Manger cancel Israel openings due to "complications"
"Putin would eat you for lunch", Harris to Trump in debate
Putin loses ally in Syria

Putin loses over 772,000 troops, 9615 tanks in war to mid-December
Puerto Rico: "floating island of garbage", Trump rally speaker
Jake Paul, 27 beat Mike Tyson, 58
Panama canal, Trump demands ownership for USA
Pink Floyd sell music rights to Sony for $400m
Plastic, biodegradable, developed in Japan
Pit Diaper, leather nappy to avoid queues for loos at gigs sells out
Lily Phillips, OnlyFans sex marathon
Porn, North Korean troops sent to Russia become addicted
Passenger Railway Services (Public Ownership) Act
Poverty rate increases in UK, year on year
Plasma jets, 23m light years long, largest seen, Lofar telescope
Prime number, largest discovered, by Luke Durant, $2^{136\,279\,841} - 1$
Gisèle Pelicot, mass rape trial
Prison exchange operation, Ankara, biggest since Cold War
Prisoner early release scheme tackles overcrowding
Prince, Starmer family's new Siberian kitten
Pumpkin, huge inflatable "attacks" Ohio police officer
Proteus, Amazon's first fully autonomous warehouse robots
Proteus robots fail to perform difficult tasks as well as humans
PopCons: Liz Truss comeback platform fails
Edwin Poots becomes Speaker of Northern Ireland Assembly
Jasmin Paris, 1st woman to complete Barkley Marathons: 100 miles in 60 hours
Piccadilly Line tests new trains
Pompeii, erotic frescoes discovered in House of Phaedra
Project 2025, Trump backers' plans
Post Office Horizon inquiry
Pigeon suspected of being Chinese spy cleared, released, Mumbai

Q
Quad-demic stresses NHS
Qilin, Russian hacking group attacks NHS
Quantum chip unveiled by Google
Qatar mediates between Israel/Hamas
Qatar suspends mediation role between Israel/Hamas
Qing Bao and Bao Li, first pandas sent China to USA in 21 years
Question Time, Farage threatens boycott over "bias"
Queen, band sell song catalogue to Sony for £1billion
Quality Street trials paper tubs
Quasar, brightest object ever discovered

R
Rise of 1.54C above global pre-industrial average
Royal family found to be charging Army, NHS rent
Royal family found to be slum landlords
Angela Rayner criticised for dancing in Ibiza
Barbara de Regil, "influencer" performs work-out mid-flight
Reform claim to have more members than Tories
RAF Scampton asylum seeker housing plan scrapped
Royal Mint's Music Legends coins: Bowie, McCartney, G. Michael & Stones.
Jim Ratcliffe of Ineos faces backlash at Manchester United
RSPCA, Caroline Lucas and Chris Packham resign

Joe Root becomes England's leading Test run-scorer
Renters' Rights Bill to end no-fault evictions
Joe Rogan claims Musk knew election result 4 hours before announced
Tommy Robinson jailed, contempt of court
Raye breaks record for most Brit Awards in single year
REO Speedwagon retire
Red diesel, illegally used on public roads during farmers' tax protests
Royal Mail sold to Czech after 500 years of British ownership
Mark Rutte becomes NATO Secretary General
Rachel Reeves becomes first female chancellor
Jacob Rees-Mogg loses seat to Labour
Ruby slippers worn in Wizard of Oz sold for $28 million
Reform UK come 2nd in 98 constituencies, gen. election
Race riots
Restore Nature Now march
Toby Roberts, GB teen wins rock climbing event, Olympics
Royal Mail stop using trains after 200 years
Rich: billionaires wealth increases by $2 trillion in 2024
Romania orders re-run of election over Russian interference
Russian election, Putin wins with 88% of vote
Republicans win control of all 3 branches of US government
Re-wilding project
Red Cross issues new language guide, branded "woke"
Rainbow lanyard ban announced by Esther McVey for civil servants
Babe Ruth's "Called Shot" jersey sold for $24.12 million
RNLI celebrates 200 years, 146,000 lives saved
Rats enjoy driving toy cars say Virginia scientists

S
Ed Sheeran complains re. vocals re-use on new Band Aid song
Sunflowers by Van Gogh targetted by Just Stop Oil again
Snoop Dogg's Olympics smoke rings pin
Synnovis ransomware, NHS cyber attack
Semaglutides, diabetes/weight loss drugs
Squirrels chemically castrated to protect trees
Sunak welches on Rwanda deportation flights bet with Piers Morgan
Sunak's election campaign calamities
Sunak threatens to axe "Mickey Mouse" degrees
Sunak on childhood struggle: "I had to go without Sky TV"
Social media to be banned for under 16s, Australia
"Sandwiches are not real food": Kemi Badenoch
Sweden becomes full member of NATO
Feargal Sharkey, clean water campaigner
Shop lifting epidemic
Sausages: Starmer mispronounces "hostages"
Gareth Southgate resigns as England manager
Brian Spencer, Southport rioter hit in head & crotch by own side's bricks
Taylor Swift, economic affect of Eras tour $10bn in USA alone
Salt Typhoon, Chinese cyber espionage attack on US
Storm Shadow, British missiles fired into Russia by Ukraine
Shipping forecast, 100th anniversary

Serco keeps failing, keeps getting govt. contracts
Scrabble, winner of Spanish world title doesn't speak Spanish
Scratch-and-sniff stamps issued by La Poste, France
Snus, nicotine pouches used by 2 in 5 pro footballers
Claudia Sheinbaum, elected first female president of Mexico
Sora, video generating AI from text
Spanish floods
Spice Girls commemorative stamp released
Skills England, body launched by Labour
RAF Scampton, no longer used to house asylum seekers
Stop the boats: Sunak's refrain
Somaliland to be recognised as official country by Trump
Sultanas shortage
Spanish entrants win Euro24 and Wimbledon
Sewage spills
Southport stabbings
Singapore Airlines Flight 321, severe turbulence, one death, 104 injured
Skibidi Toilet YouTube viral hit
Syrian rebels depose Assad
South Korean Jeju Air Boeing 737 plane crash
Arne Slot, successful replacement to Klopp at Liverpool FC
Stormzy opens #Merky FC youth centre, Croydon
Kevin Sinfield, latest fundraising, £1.2m raised, MND
Eva Marie Saint, actress reaches 100 year sold
Samba, Adidas shoes made uncool by Sunak, who "apologises"
Shrinkflation, goods getting smaller
John Swinney becomes first minister of Scotland
Santa "shot down" by Russian missile in propaganda video
Scottie Scheffler, world No.1 golfer arrested
Jay Slater, search on Tenerife

T
Trump's ear bandage copied by cultists at rally
Trump's smell: armpits, ketchup, makeup and a little butt: Adam Kinzinger
Trump's wife's naked pics shown on Russian state TV after US election
Trump sways on spot for 30 minutes to music at rally
Trump sells bibles, gold sneakers and endless gaudy tat
Trump wins election with less than 50% of vote
Terminally Ill Adults (End of Life) Bill
"Try the Battle of the Somme": Lee Anderson on hardships men v. women
Tea bags found to release microplastics into body
Justin Timberlake drink driving arrest
Trump admires Arnold Palmer's penis
Tapeworm eggs found in man who ate undercooked bacon, USA
Liz Truss pranked with lettuce banner during appearance
Tupperware files for bankruptcy after 78 years
Trees of Hope, 49 recipients of Sycamore Gap saplings
David Tennant v. Kemi Badenoch in trans row
Tomato farm lamps mistaken for Northern Lights by Dee Harrison
Thames Water troubles
Tourist backlash, Spain, Greece etc.

Anti-trans – Trump campaign's $215m ad blitz
Taiwan 7.4 magnitude earthquake, biggest in 25 years
Alan Titchmarsh's jeans censored by North Korean TV
Typhoo tea brand sold after 121 years to vape and batteries maker
Two tier policing accusation
Teachers receive pay rise
TikTok banned by US Supreme Court over security fears
Tesla lost over $94 billion in market valuation in the first two weeks of 2024
3G switch off begins
Greta Thunberg arrested at protests, Hague, Brussels
Texts sent to black Americans saying "selected to become a slave "
Twenty mph limit in Wales leads to 35% fewer deaths year on year
Teacherless AI classroom opens, David Game College, London

U

UFOs seen over New Jersey & elsewhere
Ukraine
UK suspends some arms sales to Israel
Undersea communications cables severed, Russia suspected
UK named one of the most nature-depleted countries in the world
Umbrella held by Sunak's wife during resignation speech
United Nations, impotence re. Middle East
UK Statistics Authority criticises Tory claims of tax cuts
Unexplained Aerial Phenomena, other name for UFOs
University tuition fees increase announced
Unleashed: Boris Johnson's book flops
USB-C, universal charger law, EU
Oleksandr Usyk, beats Tyson Fury twice
ULEZ expansion leads to 21% drop in pollutants
Union busting, Amazon accused
United Airlines, body found in wheel well, Maui
Universal breakfast clubs, schools trial
Uzbekistan, lost Silk Road cities discovered
United Utilities pours millions of litres of raw sewage into Lake Windermere
Upano Valley lost cities discovered, Ecuador
Undershaft, London, highest skyscraper approved
Ultra-processed foods

V

Villa Vie Residences, offers 4 year cruise to escape Trump presidency
Valencia floods, King Felipe booed and pelted with mud
Vegan scones, National Trust, unhinged fuss about "wokery"
VAT to be levied on private schools
VAT on SEND schools unfair say parents
J D Vance, Vice President-Elect seems to vanish after election
Voyager 1, 47 year old spacecraft, contact re-established by NASA
Vapes, single use ban announced
UnitedHealthcare CEO Brian Thompson shot by Luigi Mangione
Vanuatu earthquakes
Max Verstappen, wins fourth F1 world title
Vendée Globe, solo, round-the-world yacht race
Venezuela, disputed election results

Valeriana, Mayan city discovered, Mexico
Paula Vennells, Post Office inquiry
Venice tourist tax introduced
Leo Varadkar resigned as Taoiseach

W

Water companies deliver terrible service, hike prices, take bonuses
Charlie Woods, Tiger's son, hits hole in one, PNC Championship
West Bank
WallyGator, emotional support animal stolen, released in swamp
Weather app from BBC incorrectly forecast hurricanes worldwide
Winter fuel allowance means tested
Westminster honeytrap scandal
Weight loss drugs
Prince William accused of being slum landlord
Willy Wonka Experience disaster, Glasgow
Johnny Walker retires from radio
Wicked doll packaging mistakenly features link to porn site
Willow, Google's new quantum computer chip
Tim Walz, vice-presidential nominee
Prince William pledges to end rough sleeping
Geert Wilders wins the Dutch election
William Wragg, Tory MP in Westminster honeytrap scandal
Justin Welby, Archbishop resigns over abuse scandal
Wham!, first act to have Xmas No1 two years in a row
Robbie Williams planning to resit his GCSEs
Andrew Windsor's connections to an alleged Chinese spy
Greg Wallace, MasterChef, behaviour allegations
Wagatha Christie: Rooney/Vardy tribulations continue
"Wokery" added to the Oxford English Dictionary
WASPI women refused compensation
WHO records attacks on healthcare facilities, Gaza
Wiring map of brain, world first, fruit fly
War crimes, Israel/Gaza
World's hottest day, July 22 2024: NASA
World's second and third hottest days July 21 & 23 2024: NASA
Andrew Lloyd Webber has poltergeist exorcised from house
Andrew Lloyd Webber, owner of 5000 acres joins farmer IHT protest
Steve Witherden MP told off for drinking milk in Commons chamber
Wind farms onshore, Labour lifts Tory ban
Wildfires, South Africa, Greece etc.
Waitrose wonky billboard fenced off over public safety concerns

X

XL bully dogs banned
XL bully cats, experts advise against buying mutant breed
X referred to in media as "X (formerly known as Twitter)"
X loses 75% of value since Musk took over
X experiences largest ever exodus of users after election
Hongchi Xiao, slapping therapist convicted over deaths
Xi Jinping

Y
Youth Mobility Scheme discussed with EU
Yang Tenbo, suspected Chinese spy, connected to Prince Andrew
Humza Yousaf steps down as Scotland's First Minister
Yuna, shell-shocked lioness rescued from Ukraine
Yorkie and Breakaway biscuit bars discontinued by Nestle
Lamine Yamal, 17, football's highest transfer value increase

Z
Volodymyr Zelenskyy
Zig, Zimbabwe currency loses almost half its value
Zombie knife ban
Zoom call, Just Stop Oil activists arrested, jailed
"Zing and zap", Johnson praises Badenoch on becoming Tory leader

Printed in Dunstable, United Kingdom